Cultural Conflict
and Struggle

Rethinking Childhood

Joe L. Kincheloe and Janice A. Jipson
General Editors

Vol. 5

PETER LANG
New York • Washington, D.C./Baltimore • Boston
Bern • Frankfurt am Main • Berlin • Vienna • Paris

Patricia Ruggiano Schmidt

Cultural Conflict and Struggle

Literacy Learning in a Kindergarten Program

PETER LANG
New York • Washington, D.C./Baltimore • Boston
Bern • Frankfurt am Main • Berlin • Vienna • Paris

Library of Congress Cataloging-in-Publication Data

Schmidt, Patricia Ruggiano.
Cultural conflict and struggle: literacy learning
in a kindergarten program / Patricia Ruggiano Schmidt.
p. cm. — (Rethinking childhood; v. 5)
Includes bibliographical references (p.) and index.
1. Children—New York (State)—Language—Case studies.
2. Kindergarten—Social aspects—New York (State)—Case studies.
3. Asian-American children—Education—New York (State)—Case studies.
4. Socialization—New York (State)—Case studies. 5. Education, Bilingual—
New York (State)—Case Studies. 6. Multicultural education—New York
(State)—Case studies. I. Title. II. Series.
LB1181.S36   372.21'8—dc21   96-54246
ISBN 978-0-8204-3757-6
ISSN 1086-7155

Die Deutsche Bibliothek-CIP-Einheitsaufnahme

Schmidt, Patricia Ruggiano:
Cultural conflict and struggle: literacy learning in a kindergarten program /
Patricia Ruggiano Schmidt. −New York; Washington, D.C./Baltimore; Boston;
Bern; Frankfurt am Main; Berlin; Vienna; Paris: Lang.
(Rethinking childhood; Vol. 5)
ISBN 978-0-8204-3757-6
NE: GT

Cover design by James F. Brisson
Illustrations by Elva Beckmann Ruggiano

The paper in this book meets the guidelines for permanence and durability
of the Committee on Production Guidelines for Book Longevity
of the Council of Library Resources.

© 1998, 2002, 2003, 2007 Peter Lang Publishing, Inc., New York
29 Broadway, 18th Floor, New York, NY 10006
www.peterlang.com

Printed in the United States of America.

This book is dedicated to Peley, Raji, Mrs. Starr, and all who celebrate cultural diversity.

Contents

Acknowledgments

The ideas that serve as a foundation for this book came from numerous, children, families, teachers, and researchers who have been cited throughout. I am grateful for their lives and work as well as the many other wonderful people whom I acknowledge on this page.

My mentors in the Reading and Language Arts Center at Syracuse University, Professors Harold Herber, Kathleen Hinchman, Susan Hynds, Donald Leu, and Peter Mosenthal acted as exemplary teacher/researcher models. Robert Bogdan, Professor of Cultural Foundations of Education and Sociology at Syracuse University, taught me about qualitative research and reminded me that this was an important story for publication. My friend Dr. Ann Watts Pailliotet of Whitman College gave me helpful criticism and laughter throughout the entire research and writing process. My colleagues at Le Moyne College, Education Department, especially Dr. Cynthia DeCorse, encouraged me with unabashed praise. Anthony Fitchue, Le Moyne College Director of Multicultural Affairs, analyzed and discussed recommendations and suggestions offered in Chapter 7. Michele Mecomonaco and Beverly Lockwood, Le Moyne Staff, formatted, and printed.

This book also has been influenced by life experiences. Samuel Ruggiano, my father, carpenter, and labor union leader, taught me about injustice and discrimination at an early age. His struggles left me with lifelong concerns related to issues of equality and fairness.

Finally, Elva Beckmann Ruggiano, my mother, solved yet another problem. I wanted illustrations for this story, but could not see what would be appropriate. When Mother, whose avocation, for many years, has been painting and drawing, suggested pen and ink sketches, the notion seemed perfect. I asked her to create them from descriptions in the text. She replied without hesitation and completed the scenes within a week. I think her renditions give just enough information to extend the reader's visualizations of the conflicts and struggles in this kindergarten program.

Last, and the most important influence on my productivity, is Thomas, my love. He sustained my confidence while understanding that being the spouse of an assistant professor means neglect. He gracefully worked around the book in order to spend time with me.

Preface

This story began with my interest in positive home/school connections and family literacy programs (Taylor, 1983; Teale & Sulzby, 1987; Nickse, Speicher & Buchek, 1988; Edwards, 1996). Influenced by more than twenty years of experience as an elementary teacher and reading specialist, I was curious about the transfer of children's literacy learning from these programs to school classrooms. While searching for a site to observe, it was suggested by educators in a suburban school that I explore my topic in Mrs. Starr's (all names of people and places in this story are pseudonyms) outstanding kindergarten. At that site, there were two children of participating families in the district's federally funded, family literacy program.

My first visit to East Side Elementary School occurred on a sunny, crisp September morning. I arrived forty-five minutes before school and received a warm and cheerful greeting from Mrs. Starr. She immediately took me on a tour of the kindergarten classroom and explained several colorful and developmentally appropriate learning centers. At one point in our travels, we stopped to observe a bulletin board of children's self-portraits. There, Mrs. Starr directed my attention to several crayon drawings and associated their details with typical kindergarten behaviors. She also included specific thoughts about the two children I planned to observe:

> I'm worried about Peley and Raji. I think Peley's family came from Vietnam. Raji's family is from India. Look at their portraits! They're so different! Raji draws himself as a brown muscle man; Peley draws herself as a glamorous woman with a green face and a long gown! Both children are bright and have great fine motor coordination, but they're puzzling. Their English seems okay, but they don't mix. They're not making friends. They rarely speak up in class discussions. Raji stands back and observes most class activities while Peley criticizes any student near her. Neither child brings anything from home for our daily "share time."

Mrs. Starr's concerns about Peley and Raji related to their socializing. Her perceptions seemed relevant when we consider literacy development as a social phenomenon and a major emphasis in kindergartens (Spodek, 1986; Teale & Martinez, 1989). The East Side Elementary School kindergarten program encouraged children to read, write, listen, and speak through minilessons and small group activities. Literacy learning was seen as a social process equated with classroom community building. To strengthen the process, Mrs. Starr often communicated with the families of children in her classroom and connected home and school for literacy learning. Nevertheless, she knew little about either Peley's or Raji's families.

As a teacher and researcher, I realized that many factors influence literacy learning, such as cognitive and emotional factors, socioeconomic levels and home and school cultures. But, as I considered Mrs. Starr's initial statements about Peley and Raji and their apparent social struggles, I decided to focus upon the school culture. I hoped to learn how their English literacy learning would progress during the year.

A few weeks after observing the kindergarten, I telephoned the two children's families and asked to interview them in their homes to discuss school. I discovered that Peley's family came from Southeast Asian farming villages and knew very little English. Since her birth in the United States, Peley had heard and spoken Cambodian and Vietnamese dialects and learned most of her English from television. Raji's family originated in Bombay, India. They were highly educated and fluent in spoken and written English. From birth in the United States, Raji had learned to speak Hindu, Urdu, and English.

The children's primary languages were not standard English, so they were defined as bilingual, ethnic-minority children or language-minority children (Hakuta, 1986; Nieto, 1996). Typical of many schools in the United States, Peley and Raji were expected to function in both home and school cultures using their languages appropriately. Additionally, educators at East Side Elementary assumed that the two children would easily blend or fit into the school program since they would want to be a part of the social interactions in the classroom. However, comparable to the students in *The Invisible Children* (1978), Rist's ethnography of the integration of six African American children in an all White elementary school, Peley and Raji became visible problems when their behaviors were considered unusual. Educators did not know how to help them participate positively.

Similarly, Mrs. Starr resembled the fifth grade teacher in Kidder's study, *Among Schoolchildren* (1989). Both were young women from White, middle-class backgrounds who could not understand the minority children in their classrooms. Both cared passionately about their schoolchildren, but neither considered cultural conflict and its relationship to literacy learning.

This book is an account of the cultural conflicts and struggles experienced by two children and their teacher in a kindergarten program. It is divided into eight chapters. The first chapter is an introduction to the research which informs us of the consequences when we do not work to understand and appreciate our children's cultural backgrounds. In this chapter, I also briefly explain how I studied the children, teacher, and kindergarten program. The second chapter describes the children and their families, the teacher and her colleagues, and the kindergarten program within the school setting. These details help us understand the differences that might translate into cultural conflict. The third chapter portrays the children's many unhappy social encounters in learning centers, whole-group lessons and special classes. The fourth chapter outlines the components of the formal literacy learning program and the children's progress throughout the year. The fifth chapter features classroom holidays and celebrations and demonstrates the children's confusions. The sixth chapter depicts specific struggles of the children, families, and educators when there is weak communication between home and school. The seventh chapter considers the issues and principles derived from this study of cultural conflict and struggle and makes suggestions and recommendations for classroom teachers and schools. Finally, the epilogue is the story of Mrs. Starr's efforts during the year following my study. We see and hear her actions as advocate and change agent in the classroom and school.

Before you begin reading this book, I must state that discoveries made during my exploration into this kindergarten program revealed an urgent message: We as educators, must learn to understand and connect with the diverse cultural backgrounds of children and families in our classrooms. We must do this not only for the creation of successful literacy learning environments, but also for our children's successful participation in national and global communities.

Foreword

Teaching culturally diverse students is the major challenge in American education today. It is a challenge which must be accepted. First of all, our complex society needs to recognize and appreciate the latent abilities of culturally diverse students. Secondly, as Thomas Jefferson pointed out during the formation of our country, a democratic society cannot function properly unless all of its people are educated. Thirdly, our tradition of humanism tells us that the dignity of any human being must not be eroded by ignorance. Finally, education rather than ignorance should guide human behavior.

Recognizing and accepting the challenge of educating culturally diverse students does not guarantee success. Many teachers do not have the training, the knowledge, or the tools to work with culturally diverse students. They need help. They need to know the available, workable tools that they can use to connect home and school literacies.

Patricia Ruggiano Schmidt wrote *Cultural Conflict and Struggle: Literacy Learning in a Kindergarten Program* to help committed professionals understand and connect with the diverse cultural backgrounds of children and families in American classrooms. Schmidt asserts that educators "must do this not only for the creation of successful literacy learning environments, but also, for our children's successful participation in national and global communities."

Issues treated in this book require careful analysis and discussion. Schmidt underscores this point, emphasizing that teachers need additional cultural and social knowledge as they work with increasing numbers of students from varied cultural and linguistic backgrounds. Schmidt's powerful account of the cultural conflicts and struggles experienced by two children and their teacher in a kindergarten program reminded me of Sonia Nieto's book (1996), *Affirming Diversity: The Sociopolitical Context of Multicultural Education*. Primarily, because Schmidt provides a comprehensive framework for analyzing multiple causes of school failure among subordinated groups of students. Schmidt also challenges educators to strongly consider Giroux's (1993) idea of students and teachers becoming border-crossers. When this occurs, students and teachers not only refigure the boundaries of academic subjects in order to engage new forms of critical inquiry, but they also are offered the opportunities to engage the multiple references that construct different cultural codes, experiences, and histories. In this context, a pedagogy of difference provides the basis for rethinking how the relations between the dominant and subordinate groups are organized, how such relations might be transformed in order to promote a democratic and just society. Difference in this case does not become a marker for deficit, inferiority, chauvinism, or inequality; on the contrary, it opens the possibilities for constructing pedagogical practices that deepen forms of cultural democracy that serve to enlarge moral vision. *Cultural Conflict and Struggle: Literacy Learning in a Kindergarten Program* gives educators an opportunity to reflect on what we've been doing and to think about what we need to be doing in the years ahead.

Patricia A. Edwards, Ph.D.
Professor of Teacher Education
Michigan State University

References

Giroux, H.A. (1993). *Border crossings: Cultural workers and the politics of education.* New York: Routledge.

Nieto, S. (1996). *Affirming diversity: The sociopolitical context of multicultural education.* New York: Longman.

From our nation's earliest days, immigrant cultures have been encouraged to blend into the American Melting Pot.

1

Introduction: History of the Struggle

Historically, our nation's schools have functioned as the sites for socializing and preparing our children for productive roles in American society (Trueba, Jacobs & Kirton, 1990). More recently, with the influx of great numbers of Southeast Asian, Hispanic, Cuban, and Haitian refugees, this responsibility has become a demanding process (Kiefer & DeStefano, 1985) which has caused national attention to focus on children's literacy learning. Too many language-minority children do not acquire the levels of English literacy necessary for academic success in the nation's schools (Swain, 1979; Cummins, 1986; Weber, 1990). Even those children born in the United States who begin to learn English and their home languages simultaneously experience school problems (Garcia, 1994). To understand why these literacy learning problems exist, it is necessary to briefly review the assimilationist perspective, a belief that has guided education in many schools.

Assimilationist Perspective

From our nation's earliest days, immigrant cultures have been encouraged to blend into the American Melting Pot (Waggoner, 1988). Traditionally, our schools have adopted this assimilationist perspective, linking success in the United States with blending into the economic and social mainstream of society (Britton, Shafer, & Watson, 1990). Often, educators have ignored the home cultures of language-minority students in an effort to help them "fit" into the culture of the schools (Jacob & Sanday, 1976). For instance, Rodriguez (1982) and Porter (1990) explain that it is necessary for language-minority students to leave their home cultures behind if they are to be successful participants in the dominant culture represented in the schools. However, numerous studies since the 1970s have demonstrated that there are reasons why the assimilationist perspective does not promote the literacy development necessary for successful academic and social experiences (Ogbu, 1978; Paulston, 1980; Phillips, 1982; Kochman, 1983; Gumperz, 1986; Cummins, 1989; Farrell, 1991).

First, language-minority children are usually unable to reconcile the differences between home and school and become confused when they are expected to fit into the mainstream (McCaleb, 1994). Second, if the school ignores or subtracts the home culture, large portions of the children's identities must be relinquished (Cummins, 1989). Third, inappropriate classroom instruction and evaluation (Bloome, 1986; Ballenger, 1992) portray language-minority children and their families as deficient in the language abilities and cultural values of mainstream society (Cummins, 1980; Long, 1980; Moll, 1990). Therefore, in order to be successful in school, minority students must deny or make invisible significant portions of their humanity, leading them to feelings of disempowerment and loss of control in their own learning (Cardenas, 1977; Rist, 1978; Hakuta, 1986; Cummins, 1989; Fishman, 1989; Trueba, Jacobs & Kirton, 1990; McCaleb, 1994; Nieto, 1996). Consequently, the assimilationist perspective is associated with an alienation which leads to the high rate of language-minority school dropouts (Cummins, 1986; Garcia, 1994).

The remedies for this national tragedy are supported by research. It has been proposed that English literacy development occurs most effectively when language-minority students learn first to read and write in their home language (Paulston, 1980; Diaz, 1983; Rotberg,1982; Swain,1988). Schools should build upon home languages and cultures and give language-minority students the stability needed to make connections between home and school (Cummins, 1986; Kalantzis, Cope, Noble, & Poynting, 1990). If it is not possible to secure a teacher who knows the home language, then it is recommended that the school draw upon the home culture and language through the children and their families (Moll & Greenberg, 1990; Snow, 1992). For example, Swain (1972) stated in his study of bilingual literacy acquisition, "The children grow up with bilingualism as a first language," thus offering a unique opportunity in the mainstream classroom for sharing language and cultural patterns with all students. Finally, it has been reported that when language-minority children are permitted to regularly share language and culture in school, they develop their English literacy, meet success in school settings, and enliven the classroom community (Fishman, 1989; Palinscar, 1989; Goodman & Goodman, 1990; Rasinski & Padak, 1990; Resnick, 1990; Moll, 1992).

Nevertheless, many of our nation's schools continue to be firmly entrenched in the assimilation perspective and ignore diversity (Cummins,1986; Trueba, 1989; Sleeter, 1991; Miramontes, 1992). Even with the current focus on multicultural education, curriculum adaptations emphasizing the appreciation of national and world cultural diversity have not been adopted in many of our schools (Reyhner & Garcia, 1989; Flores, 1992; McCaleb, 1994; Nieto, 1996). Therefore, it appears that present and future educators need to be informed about the consequences associated with the assimilationist perspective and trained in connecting home and school for language minority literacy learning.

Early Childhood Language-Minority Literacy

The moment language-minority children begin to read and write in the majority language, the cultures of their homes can affect their success or failure in the school culture (Clay, 1971; Wong-Filmore, 1983; Verhoeven, 1987; Swain, 1988; Trueba, et al., 1990). Additionally, the quantity of majority language use in the home is not as important as the social processes related to that language at home and school (Clay, 1971; Heath, 1983; Wells, 1986; Dyson, 1989). Since research on early childhood literacy development emphasizes the social nature of literacy learning (Chomsky, 1972; Teale, 1982; Taylor, 1983; Heath, 1983; McKay, 1988; Dyson, 1989; Weber, 1990), the school and classroom teacher may guide children's literacy learning through positive social interactions. For example, Dyson's studies (1989; 1993) of communities of writers demonstrate the literacy development of children from different cultures. She states:

> What matters about writing in school is not simply the quality of the texts children produce but the quality of life they experience at school and beyond. In a community that values written language, writing can become an important means for individual reflection and social connection. And it is that feeling of belonging to a community...of connection to other people...that helps make teachers' and children's lives together personally satisfying and socially meaningful (1989, p. xvii).

It seems apparent that the classroom teacher who creates a literacy learning environment that promotes social connections and encourages the understanding of different social patterns contributes to children's literacy learning. However, the culture of many classrooms is often determined solely by classroom teachers who act as representatives of the dominant culture and are unaware of other cultures (Edwards & Mercer, 1989). They usually rely upon explicit instruction for language minority children. They directly teach the children specific classroom behaviors and evaluate literacy learning with question-answer, oral language patterns. The teacher asks the question and the student responds correctly or incorrectly (Kleifgen, 1990; Place & Becker,1991). But structured teacher-student discourse reveals little information about literacy learning, especially among minority students. Research indicates that informal classroom discourse and social interactions produce more relevant information about literacy learning in early childhood when teachers are not directly involved (Bloome & Green, 1982; Teale & Martinez, 1989).

One setting where children have numerous opportunities to informally reveal literacy learning is in the learning center (Fein, 1975; Vandenberg,1981; Gump,1989). Teachers create centers for facilitating the learning and development of a particular skill or process and intervene only when children ask for or appear to need help. Additionally, teachers may design activities which resemble or relate to the home and might be transferred to home activities (Taylor, 1983). While working and playing in centers, children examine and complete tasks as they participate cooperatively and informally in small groups (Kantor, Miller & Fernie, 1992; Neuman & Roskos, 1992). Centers actually provide the means for literacy learning as children socialize and communicate, but they may also be sites for misunderstanding when language-minority cultural differences are ignored (McCaleb, 1994). Therefore, educators must learn ways to design effective centers that connect home and school for language-minority children. Sociocultural programs in early childhood classrooms seem to be providing the means for doing just that.

Sociocultural Programs

Drawing upon home and school cultures for literacy learning is based on the sociocultural perspective, a social constructivist approach which contributes to our understanding of language-minority literacy learning (Vygotsky, 1978; 1986; Rogoff, 1986; Trueba, et al., 1990). This perspective is applied in the classroom when children construct meaning through social interactions across and within cultural settings. They become literate within the cultures of home and school (Heath, 1983; Taylor, 1983; Schiefflin & Cochran-Smith, 1984; Wells, 1986; Taylor & Dorsey-Gaines, 1988; Dyson, 1989; Moll, 1992) as they are constructing the classroom culture. The everyday life in the classroom is determined by students and teachers who elect to bring their home cultures into social interactions and contribute to the definitions of language and literacy (Green, Kantor & Rogers, 1990; Kantor, Miller & Fernie, 1992).

When studying the meanings of literacy within a classroom, sociocultural research focuses upon the complexity of developing literacy within the cultures of home and school rather than just the structural aspects of the language (Vygotsky,1978; Kaminsky, 1976; Cummins, 1986).

Recent research concerning early childhood language-minority literacy development supports the study of English from the sociocultural perspective (Snow, 1992). When language-minority parents are involved in the school culture for curriculum development and as cultural resources, there is often a narrowing of the academic gap and the development of positive attitudes (Levine, 1987; Franks, 1988; Moll, 1992; Faltis, 1993).

For example, a comprehensive study by Reyhner and Garcia (1989) clearly showed that cultural discontinuity between home and school could be practically eliminated. Parents and teachers of Polynesian, Hispanic, and Native American students from several school districts in the Southwest gathered culturally appropriate materials to engage the children in classroom activities. Within months, academic performance significantly improved.

Many sociocultural programs not only connect home and school cultures for the children in the classroom, but also include other world cultures as a natural part of daily content and process (Goldenberg,1990; Quintero&Huerto-Macias, 1990; McCaleb, 1994). Social interactions among the children encourage a sharing and celebration of differences for literacy learning.

Finally, it is clear that unsuccessful school programs for language-minority students do not connect home and school cultures. A vivid example is an ethnography by Trueba, et al. (1990), *Cultural Conflict andAdaptation: The Case of the Hmong Children in American Society*, depicting the cultural struggles of the Hmong people, refugees from Southeast Asia. During a year of participant observations in Hmong homes and public school classrooms, struggles were recorded. The Hmong students met frustration and failure in American schools. Children born in the United States especially suffered as they attempted to grow in two cultures. They were guided by an ethnocentric curriculum and experienced the feelings of cultural inferiority. The Hmong parents claimed they expected to struggle in the new land, but they did not think their children, born in America, would have to face discrimination. Hmong children stated that they were ashamed to use their home language and could not understand much of the school culture. The study's conclusions called for reform in

6

teacher education and school policy which would incorporate the sociocultural perspective for English literacy learning.

As language-minority children enter the dominant culture through the institution of the school, more relevant studies from the sociocultural perspective are needed to convince educators that connecting home and school cultures is essential (Garcia, 1986; Trueba, et al., 1990).

Additionally, since the early childhood years are critical in the development of literacy learning (Wells, 1986; Taylor & Dorsey-Gaines, 1988; Dyson, 1989), studying early childhood, language-minority literacy development helps us gain significant information about early classroom struggles (Garcia, 1986; Edelsky, 1986; Taylor & Dorsey-Gaines, 1988). From this information, changes can be made in classrooms and schools for connecting home and school cultures.

Exploring the Classroom Culture

My study of two language-minority children in a kindergarten program demonstrates the cultural conflict and struggles when home and school are not connected. I chose ethnography as the methodology to systematically describe the classroom struggles. Ethnography is "thick description" of people's perspectives in the context of a naturalistic setting (Geertz, 1973). It attempts to provide meaningful knowledge of the culture through shared interpretations. Since it offers opportunities to observe culture during extended periods of time, it provides "understanding of the meanings of socially situated actions from the actors' points of view"(Rowe, 1994).

Symbolic interactionism (Blumer, 1969) served as the theoretical framework for helping me understand Peley's and Raji's struggles as well as Mrs. Starr's struggles in the kindergarten. This framework is congruent with the social constructivist approach (Rogoff, 1986) and is based on the premise that the way people act depends on the interpretation of a situation and the meaning they give it. Literacy development in this kindergarten program consisted of meaning-making through social interactions. That meaning was derived from social interactions and modified through social process (Blumer, 1969).

As the ethnographer, I gained a panoramic view of the school setting while observing and recording the way people behave and learn within the context of the classroom culture (Lincoln & Guba, 1985; Spindler & Spindler, 1987). During the year, frequent participant observation, interviews and collection of related classroom documents produced volumes of descriptive information. As a participant observer, I became part of the kindergarten classroom environment two to three days each week and experienced "prolonged, intense social interaction while collecting data unobtrusively and systematically in the form of field notes" (Bogdan, 1972). Observations were extended to other settings such as music, library, physical education, computer lab, cafeteria, field trips, playground, parent conferences, and student homes.

Kindergarten teachers, teaching assistants, principal, high school teacher aides, classmates, the two children, and their parents were periodically interviewed. I used the open-ended, unstructured interview process (Spradley, 1979; Bogdan & Biklen, 1994) in order to give people the option to follow comfortable paths of thought. Interviews were scheduled or unscheduled when opportunities arose during participant observation. On several occasions, I met with the two children, parents, and families in their respective homes.

Finally, I collected school documents, such as materials from the literature-based series, pieces of children's literature from the classroom and school library, report cards, standardized test scores, parent conference sheets, children's school work, children's computer printouts, teacher's lesson plans, and home/school oral and written communication.

Data analysis took place in terms of qualitative practice and was ongoing from the beginning of the study. As I read and reread notes, documents and interviews, I coded and catagorized all of the information. I soon discovered patterns of social interactions and identified relationships between and among the patterns. With further exploration and data gathering, additional information strengthened the patterns and relationships which emerged as themes specifically grounded in classroom evidence (Glaser & Strauss, 1967). Following the traditions of Rist (1978) and Bloome and Green (1982), the data were so rich in detail that the study itself evolved into what seemed to be a feature-length film representation of social struggle in the context of a kindergarten program. Throughout this story, the voices of children, parents and teachers are heard using their actual words to explain their perceptions of situations.

Data collection and analyses were influenced by the perspectives gained during my years of teaching experience and professional knowledge of early childhood education, educational programs, and literacy instruction. Also, it is important to note that I have always been an outspoken advocate for children with special needs. So when the children's struggles appeared obvious, I was troubled and wondered about informing faculty, staff, and parents about multicultural instructional strategies. But, after numerous consultations with other ethnographers and reading about similar research dilemmas (Bogdan & Biklen, 1994), I decided not to share the information. There were two major reasons: (1) I believed my interpretations might be premature and unfounded, and (2) based upon readings (Taylor & Bogdan, 1984; Bogdan & Biklen, 1994) and discussions with experienced researchers, I realized that overwhelming evidence would be necessary if permanent changes would take place in the school setting. I feared that telling Mrs. Starr about my observations and concerns in November or January would indicate only isolated incidents rather than patterns of culture conflict. This was a difficult decision to make, but one in which ethnographers must wrestle in their work.

In conclusion, my own European American background and lack of contact with people of other cultures made it difficult for me to visit the children's homes. I had read about Cambodian, Vietnamese, and Indian cultures, but reading about them was not the same as stepping into their homes and actually communicating. I was nervous and afraid of saying and doing things incorrectly. I was worried that I might misinterpret the families and they might misinterpret me. It was also painful to not take a more proactive stance for the families and their children. Therefore, in order to recognize these reactions and concerns as part of data interpretation, I wrote observer comments within field notes and interviews. Additionally, my journal, in the form of memos, questions, and thoughts acted as a check on intrusive behaviors and the means for reflective thinking, thus adding to more questions and reactions (Bogdan & Biklen, 1994). Furthermore, I used Spindler and Spindler's (1987) reflective cultural analyses and interview process in order to raise my consciousness level of ethnocentricism.

Summary of the Struggle

Where cultural conflict exists, struggles abound. Since language minority children have a home culture different from the school culture, they often struggle within the White, middle class, school culture (Wong-Filmore, 1983; Verhoeven, 1987; Swain, 1988; Reyhner & Garcia, 1989; Trueba, et al., 1990). This year-long ethnography from the sociocultural perspective offers a unique view of a kindergarten program that perceived literacy learning as a social phenomenon involving home and school (Heath, 1983; Moll, 1990). The program was considered excellent by European American parents and educators in the suburban community but failed to connect home and school for language-minority students. The findings from the study contribute to our understanding of cultural conflicts in classrooms and the need for change.

The descriptions and dialogue of cultural conflict are vividly presented during formal and informal work and play settings, formal literacy learning sessions, holidays and celebrations and home and school communication. Before scenerios are examined, the children's home cultures and the school cultures are described in the next chapter, so the reader may visualize the context of this story.

Every morning before the kindergarten students arrived, groups of first and second graders from previous years stepped into Mrs. Starr's room for hugs.

2

The Setting: Home and School Cultures

Mrs. Starr, the kindergarten teacher at East Side Elementary School, began describing her concerns about Peley and Raji during my first autumn visits to the classroom. She stated:

> Peley does what she wants in learning centers. She will often ignore what she's supposed to do. She rarely smiles. She does spend a lot of time making her letters. Raji is very quiet and seems in a shell. He likes to draw. I wonder about their literacy learning.

According to kindergarten screening tests and the teacher's observations of emerging literacy, Peley and Raji were considered top students academically. However, their behaviors caused doubt about future progress. Furthermore, educators at East Side Elementary School were unaware of the children's home cultures. In order to set the stage for a clear picture of the cultural differences between home and school, this chapter describes Peley, Raji, their homes and families, Mrs. Starr, kindergarten classmates, program, school, and staff (Schmidt, 1993a).

Peley

With a serious brown face, a swishing, long black pony tail, and almond-shaped, dark eyes, an average-sized kindergarten child anxiously darted into the classroom. Her stone-washed jeans were a size too small showing her yellow socks and worn sneakers with velcro straps pressed in place. A purple belt was haphazardly looped through her jeans. A dingy pink, flowered, long-sleeved, cotton knit, turtle neck shirt was tucked into the jeans. Wavy hair was held in place with a soiled yellow and black bow. Her bangs were unevenly cut, extremely short across her forehead, revealing a bruise about the size of a quarter.

During those first weeks of kindergarten, Peley appeared to be five years and six months of unpredictable, volatile behaviors. In the morning, she would bounce into the classroom with an item from home, such as a unique clasp from her mother's Cambodian jewelry box. She might show the teacher, but not her classmates and tease, "I'm not going to show this to you. You can't see it!" The children would look at her clenched hand and then turn away from her. She might also initiate unpleasant conversations. "I don't like your shirt" or "You stink!" or "You're not my friend."

At other times, in play centers, she would attempt pleasant conversations. "Matt, I saw you on the bus. I like you. Will you be my friend?" Matt would look at her and turn his head, ignoring her plea. She would then feign illness and with tears, ask to go to the nurse while crying, "I'm sick; I hurt."

Mrs. Starr tried pairing Peley with students during work and play, but usually Peley would begin criticizing. "That letter! Messy!" or "Your picture, not good." Her laughter was loud and unexpected; her frowns and tears would arrive seconds later. When she received attention from the teacher or teacher aides, she would become quiet.

Peley's behaviors made her one of the students that Mrs. Starr considered a serious emotional problem as she planned the daily lessons. "If only she had a friend, she might feel better. I just can't figure out her problems."

Peley's Home and Family

Peley's family lived in a two-bedroom, ranch-style home with an attached one-car garage. It was part of a housing track of similar homes built in the early 1950s and sat on a fifty-by-seventy-five-feet plot of land. The light green paint on the clapboards was peeling and the precast, concrete front steps were crumbling. A faded United States flag hung on a loose and tilting wrought iron railing, the only flag visible in the neighborhood. The lawn was cut, but the yard was trimmed with overgrown weeds. A ten-feet-tall, lone, scrawny mountain ash tree stood in the middle of the front lawn. A previously owned 1986 gray-blue Dodge van occupied the gravel driveway.

Inside the house was a living room, eat-in kitchen, one bathroom and two bedrooms. The living room, decorated in tans, browns, and oranges, held two large sofas; a matching afghan adorned one of the sofas. The walls were covered with framed family and individual photos. Light blue polyester lined drapes were drawn across the picture window to keep the glare off the continually tuned television screen. Next to the television was an entertainment center which included a VCR, tape deck, radio, and stereo. An electric piano was adjacent.

Peley's parents met and married in the United States through a local church group that resettled Southeast Asian refugees. The family consisted of her Cambodian mother and grandmother, her Vietnamese father, and her elder brother, by one year, Johnny.

Grandmother had recently arrived from California, where she had been living with her second daughter.

Peley's parents were usually dressed in dark cotton slacks and short-sleeved T-shirts. This was the standard work attire in the local medical instrument's factory where her father worked night shifts and her mother worked days. The job was secure, and Peley's mother talked openly about finances.

> We get good job. Extra work on weekend. We own home. We get mortgage. Rent no good. We live apartment, city. No good.

Peley's grandmother was most often seen in a loose fitting cotton, flowered housecoat or dress. She was the member of the household who brought tea and cookies to guests while bowing and speaking Cambodian. Her main household tasks were cooking and helping the children get ready for school in the mornings.

The family socialized exclusively with several Cambodian cousins and friends who lived in the area. On special weekends, when the parents were not working, they exchanged visits and invited relatives and friends to stay the night rolled up in blankets on the living room floor. Since Peley and Johnny did not play with children in the neighborhood, their mother explained, "Peley and Johnny have cousins. Weekend, see cousins."

Peley and her brother spoke English without a hint of another language. Even though they could understand and speak their father's Vietnamese dialect, they often chose to communicate with their parents and grandmother in a Cambodian dialect and alternated answers in English and Cambodian. Peley's mother was more fluent in English than her father and openly declared, "Husband, no learn English. He no like." Consequently, letters from school were rarely understood by the children or the family. When I visited their home during the school year, the mother would bring out the messages about physical checkups, immunization, and any special meetings for translation.

Peley's father was the family representative for most school functions, because of his availability during the school day. Due to his lack of sleep and limited English, notes from school were frequently misinterpreted. He might appear at the kindergarten door days or hours late for functions or appointments. Nevertheless, both parents desperately wanted their children to be literate. Peley's mother explained,

> Cambodia, school cost money. People, not read. Not like United State.

United State education free! Peley and Johnny go to school. Peley and
Johnny read!

Peley's parents supported the school program with
snacks, school visits and trips to the public library. Her
mother saw Peley outperforming her brother, Johnny. She
stated emphatically,

Peley tell us. She learn English. She work. Not like Johnny. Johnny
lazy. Like my husband. English, not good.

Peley was the member of the family with the best grasp of
English. She was the one who answered the phone and took
messages. When I visited the home, her mother and grandmother
watched with smiles as she read to me and talked about school.

Raji

Raji's eyes dominated his ebony, satin face as he calmly
walked into the classroom. They were dark saucers with lashes
and eyebrows, thick and silky. His soft, wavy hair framed his
face and was cut to his round, small ears. You were hardly
conscious of his straight, tiny nose, because his serious mouth also
caught one's attention. Raji was smaller than the average
kindergarten student. His too short, black, cotton trousers
revealed white socks and gray, velcro-strapped sneakers. His
black and red heavy winter sweater was typical attire, no matter
what the temperature indoors or out. Each morning, during the
first weeks of school, Raji sat alone on the red rug, waiting for
attendance to begin and rarely initiating social interactions.
While making letters in clay, at the writing center, Raji often made
snake "S". When asked about his snake, he began telling about all
the snakes that lived around his friend's home. The students
reacted with sounds and words of revulsion, "Yuck! Don't say
it!", "Ugh! Terrible!", "I hate it!" Raji's talk would be brought to a
halt. Later, it was discovered that he had been referring to the
snakes seen at his friend's home in India.
When Mrs. Starr asked Raji questions, he answered in ways
which seemed to indicate that he did not understand the question.
A teacher-led discussion concerning the meaning of surprise
occurred in a small group. Mrs. Starr asked, "Raji, have you ever
been surprised?" Raji answered, "Yes." She continued. "Can
you tell us when?" He responded, "When I had muscleman
toothbrush. He is strong." Raji had received the toothbrush as a

surprise gift from his father, but Mrs. Starr was only aware of the muscleman self-portrait. She looked at Raji quizzically and turned to another student to ask the question. Later in the day, Mrs. Starr commented, "Sometimes, he just doesn't seem to be with us. I can't figure him out."

Raji's Home and Family

Raji's family lived in a modern apartment complex that housed families from a variety of ethnic and socioeconomic backgrounds. Large, two-story, rectangular-shaped, dark, wooden-shingled buildings were scattered methodically over several street blocks. An Olympic-sized swimming pool and tree-shaded play areas surrounded Raji's building. His home was one of the eight apartments found in each structure. Entrance into his family's home occurred through a small dimly lit interior hallway. The door possessed a small peep hole and push button bell. It opened into the family living room.

Upon entering the apartment, the first sight was the portable television dominating the wall opposite a large tan sofa. A small wooden coffee table sat in front of the sofa with children's art work and crayons scattered about. Partially drawn beige drapes covered a wall with sliding glass doors leading to a small wooden balcony porch. It stored a plastic big-wheel bike and other assorted brightly colored plastic toys.

The kitchen was across the room from the sliding doors and held a small table squeezed against one wall. A stove, sink and refrigerator lined the opposite wall. There was barely enough room for two adults to stand in between.

Raji's parents came to the United States from an area near Bombay, India. His father graduated as an engineer from a prestigious Indian university and earned a master's degree in business from a famous university in the northeastern United States. Raji's father sent for his bride, Raji's mother, a year after his arrival. The marriage had been arranged when they were children. Raji and his sister, Deet, three years of age, were born in the United States.

Raji's father dressed in slacks and sport shirt, the appropriate clothing for an engineer working in a large local company. He walked to work daily, so their late model compact automobile could serve as transportation for Raji's mother. Daily, she studied for her high school diploma in the United States. She usually wore slacks, cotton blouses, and cardigans. A diamond stud was also occasionally worn on the side of one nostril.

The family social life revolved around other Indian families in the university area, but Raji's parents expressed an interest in socializing with people born in the United States. Sadly though, Raji's father explained that their social encounters with Americans had not developed, "They invite us to dinner; we invite them to dinner and then it ends. I don't understand. We want to know them."

Raji's parents supported the school program and encouraged him to do well academically. They worked at home to improve his reading, writing, and speaking. Their spoken English was excellent, but Raji's father apologized for his British pronunciations of some words. They understood messages from school and attended all special meetings. When they visited their families in India, they asked for Raji's school work so he wouldn't fall behind. Raji's parents were also concerned that he did not have friends in school and wanted him to actively participate. Raji's father stated,

> We came to the United States by choice and expected some difficulties. Raji was born here. He is an American. Why can't he make friends? Why should he struggle?

Mrs. Starr

Mrs. Starr's gentle manner was accented by her soft, blond, shoulder-length hair, slightly curled at the ends. Her face showed a creamy pink complexion with large brown eyes set to peer into children's minds. A clear delicate voice enunciated words perfectly and a smiling mouth often broke into deep strong laughter. Her twenty-six years of age barely seemed possible. She was a trim, five feet two inches tall and wore fashionably, loose fitting, clothing in subtle colors, trimmed with gold accessories. One inch heels gave her walk an authoritative click.

Every morning before the kindergarten students arrived, groups of first and second graders from previous years stepped into Mrs. Starr's room for hugs. They shyly answered her questions about their homes and families and then left to begin their day in another part of the school.

Mrs. Starr originated from Long Island where she grew up in an upper middle-class community. Her family was college educated. While in high school, she dreamed of attending an Ivy League school, but her father's untimely death limited family resources. She graduated from a state university, receiving a degree in elementary education. She met her husband while in college; they married soon after graduation and settled in his home town, a suburb near East Side Elementary School. Both were presently working on their master's degrees in education.

Mrs. Starr was considered an excellent teacher and leader by the staff at East Side Elementary. She was involved in professional development committees and had helped to bring new ideas and programs to the school. She was a tireless professional who arrived in school an hour before the other teachers and left two hours after the day ended. Whenever a problem or success occurred in the classroom, she usually reflected and shared with other staff members. As a result, she always seemed to be searching for better ways of teaching and learning.

During the kindergarten year, Mrs. Starr kept tuned to her students strengths and needs. If she had any questions about academic or social performance, she would contact a specialist within the school and confer with the respective family. She seemed to understand most of her students' family situations; if there were any significant changes in behaviors, her professional and intuitive sense guided her to take action with a phone call, a note home and or a school conference. When Mrs. Starr first noticed Peley's and Raji's social struggles, she tried to help them in the classroom in all the ways her training, experiences, and time allowed, but nonetheless, their year's journey through kindergarten was marked with frustrations and struggles. Mrs. Starr struggled too.

Kindergarten Classmates

Shades of blond hair and blue eyes dominated the student population at East Side Elementary School. In the three kindergarten classrooms, there were only five students of color. Three were African American; Raji and Peley were the remaining two.

Clothing was an important part of the kindergarten culture; the students had numerous outfits. The boys usually wore popular brands of trousers and jeans with shirts imprinted with names of favorite athletic teams or pictures of cartoon characters. Advertized expensive sneakers were standard wear. The girls donned stirrup pants and oversized bright sweaters, flowery coordinated tops and bottoms and the latest Disney apparel reflecting current movies and toys. Sneakers, leather strapped flats, and lacy leotards were common. Peley and Raji dressed in the same few outfits throughout the school year.

In the morning, groups of boys and girls gathered around the room before attendance on the red rug. One group might consist of girls discussing new clothing. A second group might be boys and girls showing toys or objects brought for sharing. A third group could be seated in and around the story chair with one child reading a book while others listened. Finally another group might be on the rug waiting for attendance and quietly chatting. Boys and girls mingled freely. Many were from the same neighborhoods. Raji and Peley were rarely part of any group.

The Kindergarten Program

School administrators, faculty, and parents described the East Side Elementary School morning and afternoon kindergarten programs as excellent. The literacy program was created and developed by a team of tenured kindergarten teachers with less than ten years experience. The preschool teaching assistant and computer teaching assistant worked with the team and were considered major contributors. The administration had advertised the half-day programs as outstanding, because they cultivated the necessary experiences for a kindergarten population lacking print awareness. Literacy learning was based on a variety of activities located in nine learning centers divided among the three kindergarten classrooms. Stories and poems read by the teachers provided themes for attentive listening, class discussions, field trips, language experience stories and development of fine and gross motor coordination. Activities occurred continuously in fifteen to twenty minute intervals throughout the two-and-one-half-hour morning and afternoon sessions. The last half hour of each program, three days a week, was devoted to physical education, music or library.

A new literature-based reading program was the framework for formal reading instruction and provided a variety of children's literature and a sequence of specific reading and writing skills. There was also a language component in this program that was separated from the literature-based reading component. A computer-assisted, writing-to-read program and small group language arts instruction occurred daily.

An important ingredient in the morning kindergarten program was the high school early childhood education program. Four female, at-risk high school students spent the mornings working as teacher aides in the three classrooms. During afternoons, they attended academic classes at the high school. They were assigned to a specific kindergarten teacher and supervised by the preschool teaching assistant. As aides, they studied child development and helped with lesson preparations by creating theme bulletin boards and kindergarten learning games. They were also trained to read aloud to the children and help the children complete assigned tasks in several of the learning centers. As a result, the high school assistants learned about emerging literacy and played a significant role in the morning kindergarten routine.

East Side Elementary School and Staff

East Side Elementary School was located in a village which historically housed White American working-class and immigrant families. It was a neighborhood school with kindergarten through grade two, one of five elementary schools within a large suburban school district in northeastern United States. The tan cement facade of the two-story square structure was decorated with Greek revival scroll work and carvings. The architecture resembled buildings constructed in the late 1930s. About one hundred feet directly opposite the main entrance, an American flag waved high upon a pole surrounded with circular cement sidewalks. Every morning, no matter what the weather, before the bell rang, children could be seen chasing around it. The large front lawn area contained several locust and maple shade trees, completing the picture of a school in small town U.S.A.

The large, modern, gray-tinted glass windows of the building were an obvious recent renovation. They were usually adorned with symbols of a coming holiday or event. In the late sixties, a red brick one-story module on the back, left side of the main structure was added to house the kindergarten. It was sheltered and shaded by a giant maple tree.

Walking through the front entrance of the school, the first impression was solid construction and perfect maintenance. The shiny, warm, cream brick and ceramic walls and dustless block marble floors squeaked with cleanliness. Children's drawings and writing pieces were neatly displayed everywhere.

The faculty parking lot, off to the side of the school, was filled with expensive, foreign-made automobiles; most of the teachers were women and did not live in the school neighborhood. The principal, a stately, slender, tall woman in her early forties, commanded respect when she entered a room. Her bright eyes focused completely on the person who was speaking or listening. She possessed a rosy complexion, blue eyes and light auburn, softly curled hair. The female staff in the building resembled her physically even though most were younger and shorter. They also usually dressed in conservative skirts and slacks with silk blouses and neat knits. Gold earrings and chains were tastefully worn as accents.

The men on the faculty and staff were about ten years older than the women. The physical education teacher, music teacher, reading teacher, and janitor appeared to be in their late forties or early fifties. They had no particular common physical characteristics, but they all appeared intensely interested in performing their jobs well.

The physical education teacher modeled activities for the children and laughed heartily. The music teacher prepared lessons which rivaled any educational children's program on television. The reading teacher seemed absolutely absorbed in the importance of children's reading progress. Since he was the major diagnostician in the school, he kept meticulous records of all examinations and grouped students for each grade. The janitor was openly proud of the exemplary condition of the school.

Based on socioeconomic factors, the school qualified for a large array of federally funded material, equipment, and programs which served to enrich the educational setting. The faculty seemed to perceive the children who came to this school as deprived of material possessions as well as parental support for learning. Therefore, programs were designed to fill in knowledge gaps believed necessary for success in the school's learning environment. Field trips and student active involvement in the learning process were promoted.

Also, many events were planned to bring parents to school. They were asked to visit, help in the classrooms, and participate in special events and activities. Homework was also designed to encourage parental assistance.

Peley and Raji were not the first language-minority children to progress through East Side Elementary. The English-as-a-second-language (ESL) teacher worked with students for each grade level in a pull-out program, during two thirty-minute periods a week. The principal explained that their ESL Program was above minimum standards required by the government. She also emphasized that they rarely had any problems associated with language-minority students.

Education was celebrated at East Side Elementary. During daily morning announcements, names of students receiving perfect test scores, special awards and student pieces of writing were read by children, teachers, and principal. Additionally, perpetual smiles on the faces of staff members appeared to be an outward trademark of their enjoyment of teaching and caring for children. They were proud of this school and believed the community could take pride in what was happening there.

Summary of Settings

Even though the East Side Elementary School Program was considered excellent by the community, Peley, Raji, and Mrs. Starr experienced a year of cultural conflict and struggle. The children's families anxiously and quietly suffered at home in a state of confusion. They had great respect for education and realized that their children were capable students. They wanted their children to do well but saw their children as extremely unhappy. The next chapter portrays the disturbing social interactions experienced by Peley and Raji during work and play in learning centers, whole group lessons, and special classes.

During most of the year, classmate interactions lacked a positive tone for Peley and Raji. Neither child seemed able to successfully gain entry into the group.

3

Isolation: Working and Playing With Others

The sociocultural perspective views literacy in terms of culture; children become literate in their family, community, and classroom cultures. Furthermore, social interactions within the classroom culture often demonstrate literacy learning. (Kantor, et al., 1992). Similarly, Mrs. Starr and the other kindergarten teachers perceived literacy learning as a social phenomenon which permeated every aspect of the kindergarten program. The children were encouraged to socialize for the enhancement of their reading, writing, listening, and speaking. However, research suggests that because language-minority children have a home culture different from the school culture, they may not understand social interactions within the classroom culture. Consequently, their literacy learning may be adversely affected (Trueba,et al., 1990).

Both Peley and Raji appeared to struggle as they worked and played with classmates during the school year. Their struggles were noticed by Mrs. Starr as early as the first weeks of school and labeled as unusual for kindergarten students. She believed this would change and looked for ways to help Peley and Raji acquire friends. Throughout the school year, she asked them who they would like to work or play and placed them in a variety of situations with different students. She openly praised them in front of their classmates for special talents and accomplishments. "Peley, you can read a lot of words," or "Raji, you make great pictures." Finally, she selected them for student leadership roles. But Peley seemed to turn potential friends away, because of her voliatile behaviors and negative criticisms. Raji stayed to himself. When he did attempt to share, students gave negative responses. Mrs. Starr was puzzled and concerned, but was unable to understand the emerging patterns as Raji and Peley worked and played in the classroom.

The following typical scenes depict the children's social interactions during whole group lessons and small group learning centers (Schmidt, 1995).

Pretty Red Rug

In the morning opening ceremonies, the children gathered on

the oriental style, "pretty red rug" for attendance, pledge, announcements and weather check. The rug was located between two sets of shelves holding large wooden building blocks on one side and small boxes of plastic blocks on the other. The children knew they were not allowed to play with items on the shelves during that time and directed their attentions to the large calendar on the wall facing them. Removable laminated numbers for the days of the week, names of the days and months were held on small metal cup hooks. There were also weather symbols hung on another hook, so the children could select rainy, snowy, cloudy, windy or sunny when deciding the weather for the day. Weekly, selected student names appeared next to the "busy bees," laminated bumble bees. These children performed daily tasks and errands. One student took the attendance to the office and was allowed to choose a buddy to go with him or her. Another child placed all of the calendar and weather items in their proper places with the help of the teacher and the rest of the class. Finally one child held the flag and led the class in the Pledge of Allegiance.

Patterns of negative social interaction emerged in this setting. There was a lot of conversation during that time of the day, but Peley and Raji were usually not involved. The children would be seated cross-legged in twos or threes on the rug. Raji would enter the classroom and go directly to his position. He would sit with arms folded on the rug next to the teacher's chair. Occasionally, he would gaze at a group to his left, seeming to listen intently.

Raji visited relatives in India during December and January. Before he left, there was no mention in the classroom about his trip. When he returned after two months, he skipped into the classroom and began initiating conversations. He questioned, "Do you like Barney? I do. Dinosaurs are great. I have a collection. Do you want to see them in my pockets? Can you say their names?" Students responded with "So what!" or "Who cares!" or "How come you weren't here?" Within two weeks, Raji withdrew, isolated again on the red rug.

In the morning, Peley would bounce into the classroom and briefly converse with the teacher. She would show Mrs. Starr a clasp for her pony tail, an empty bottle of perfume, harmonica, comb or a small jewelry item from from Southeast Asia. Mrs. Starr would ask questions about them. Peley would quickly answer and hide her treasures in a pocket. Then, she would sit alone toward the back of the group. One day she loudly asked

Vanessa, "Hi, will you be my friend?" Several children turned around. Peley continued, "I have something in my pocket." Some children ignored her, and others looked at her quizzically. Vanessa responded, "You are too loud! Go away! Who wants to see your funny stuff!"

When Peley talked with the boys, the remarks were often bathroom oriented and inappropriate. "Your shirt has doo doo on it! Oh! yucky!" She would get immediate negative verbal responses from some of the boys. "Oh shut up! You're yucky!"

Another example of Peley's social interaction occurred when Veronica and Vanessa were sitting where Peley usually sat. Peley commanded, "Get up Veronica, you sit in my place!" Her harsh command was obeyed instantly. Veronica and Vanessa quickly moved to the opposite end of the rug.

Busy bee buddy selection demonstrated additional evidence of negative patterns. Children were allowed to choose friends to go on errands in other parts of the school. The students giggled and quickly named a friend. When Peley was "busy bee," she would spend inordinate amounts of time for selections and would finally choose someone most often named by other students. Peley was rarely chosen as someone's buddy. When Raji was "busy bee," he called on Jerry, a soft-spoken, blonde, blue-eyed child or Ashton, the African American child. Jerry would occasionally choose Raji. However, Peley and Raji spent most of the year alone on the "pretty red rug."

Whole Group Lessons

Patterns of social interaction for Peley and Raji were consistently negative whenever the whole group met for minilessons in language or math. The lessons always had follow-up activities at the small round tables; Peley rarely sat where she wanted. She would approach a table, begin to sit and a student would say, "No, this is for Lisa" or "Matt is sitting here" or "You can't sit here." Peley would wander from table to table until Mrs. Starr would tell her where to sit or she would find a place where no one objected. When she was finally seated, she would begin her criticism of the student work being produced around her. Comments were, "That is messy," or "That doesn't look like a bear," or "You aren't doing that right." While studying dominoes in a math lesson, she reprimanded, "You count them this way! You can't put them there! You have to look at them and count them."

Raji usually found a place at one of the tables quickly and

quietly and went to work without looking left or right. He rarely spoke or was spoken to by the children. While other students would ask for help or approval from the teacher, he waited silently for the teacher to come around. Toward the end of the year, if Jerry or Peley sat at his table and he needed help, Raji could be heard saying "What do we do?" or "I don't know this."

Both Peley and Raji did not have the positive exchanges experienced by other children at their tables. Typical recorded comments were "Let me see your bear!" or "Your bear is funny and smiling," or "I like to count these," or "I like to make a house with these dominoes," or "This is fun!"

Learning Centers

Patterns of interaction at the nine learning centers in this kindergarten program also demonstrated the struggles of the two children. Daily, the class went to the learning center board to discover their new assigned centers located in the three classrooms. Children worked and played with their own classmates as well as others from the kindergarten rooms. Teachers regularly changed the composition of groups to make opportunities for new friends.

The centers had a weekly nursery rhyme or alphabet theme. Each center had a teacher-assisted task or "work" which was to be completed first. Then the children played, defined by the teacher as any child-initiated activity using materials in the center. All types of scenarios for individuals, pairs, or groups were created. Imagination and experimentation produced dramatizations, unique art and architecture, mechanical wonders, stories, and poems. Nevertheless, during center times, Raji was usually dominated by the other students. Peley dominated others and was critical of students in the group. For no apparent reasons, Peley and Raji were rarely placed in centers together. The following are descriptions of the learning centers and examples of typical recorded social interactions for the two children.

Sand and Water Center. This center was a large plastic and wooden 2' x 3' table on wheels. Children were given plastic containers or toys related to the weekly kindergarten theme. Peley would often behave wildly at this table. She would scream and laugh as she poured water out of a jug, saying that it reminded her of bathroom functions. She would smash sand castles, splash water and tend to make the rest of the group angry. Sometimes, students would frantically call for help from the teaching assistant. By the end of the year, Peley wasn't as boisterous. Instead she would accomplish the destruction of her own creations without calling attention to herself.

Raji would play quietly in a corner of the table. He would make a suggestion. "Let's make a waterfall." or "Let's put a tower on that." He was either ignored or emphatically opposed. "We don't need that!" or "No, that's not right!" Quietly, he would stay in his corner and play alone while the other three continued with a project. No teacher, assistant, or aide were near the center to intervene.

Readiness Center. This center contained a large variety of games which examined grapheme-phoneme connections, phonological awareness, and fine motor coordination. Students also studied a variety of puzzles, shoe-tying, and tools like wrenches, screw drivers, and mallets. Peley would do everything possible to win any game played in the center. She would insist on having a second spin in order to get the number of spaces needed to win. She would take extra time to use a tool, so she could finish her project before another child. She would even insist that they were putting a puzzle together incorrectly. "You do it wrong. I can do it!" or "Give me another turn! See I win!" During the year, she had only one student actually confront her. Kristie, from another class, would challenge Peley, "No! It's not your turn. You had a turn! You have to wait!" Usually, the resulting verbal commotion signaled a need for help. A teaching assistant would reprimand both children for their loudness and inability to share. Peley, however, would retreat with a pout and not continue to play.

Another instance clearly demonstrated Peley's struggles related to culture. When the theme for the week was the letter "H", the game was to say words with the letter. Peley mentioned, "I have two H's in my name." Kristie responded, "No, you don't! Say your name." Peley answered, "Peley Lom Chinh, Peley Lom Chinh! C-h-i-n-h!" The other children ignored them and went on with the game. Kristie added, "No you don't! I don't hear hu, hu, hu." Peley withdrew with frowning face, folded arms, and head bent. She was always known as Peley Lom on the large classroom primary paper roster printed for attendance. The name Chinh had never been formally used in school even though it appeared on her official school records. Peley and her family were unable to explain the cultural significance of their two last names Lom and

Chinh, so the school had ignored one.

Raji had difficulties at the readiness center with tying shoestrings. He wore velcro-strap sneakers and seemed unaware of the importance of learning to tie laces. When the tie games appeared, he urgently asked to go to the bathroom. At the end of the school year, when Mrs. Starr informed Raji's parents of this deficiency, they were amazed. In India, where tie shoes were not typical for children, this was an unusual school requirement.

Raji found success in other activities at the center. He patiently manipulated the screw driver and wrench and could spend twenty minutes attempting to put together one or two plastic pieces with large plastic bolts. When it was "M" week, he was introduced to a matching game, similar to one he played at home from India. His quiet response after being given the directions by the teaching assistant was, "This is a memory game. You need to remember what is under the pictures." His remarks went unheard; he proceeded to win the game easily. The other children continued playing long after his victory. Rather than recognize his victory, they focused on each other and the game. Again, no teacher was present to hear or see the interchange.

Housekeeping Center. This center had a kitchen containing cabinets, sink, stove, refrigerator, closet, and crib. Aprons, baby clothes, table linens, dishes, plastic food and cleaning equipment were included in the dramatization of domesticity. A child could be ironing, cooking, serving dinner, washing dishes, sweeping, tending the baby doll, or sitting at the table. Students moved around performing tasks of their choosing with some talk. "What do we have for dinner?" or "Leftovers again!" or "Dinner is ready!" or "The baby is awake" or "I better iron." Raji sat at the kitchen table or hung back and watched the other students taking various roles as mother, father, sister, or brother.

There was a full-length ruffled apron in the broom closet worn by the designated mother. Peley would insist on being the mother and usually get her way, unless Kristie was in the group. Then Peley would settle for the sister role. In this center, Peley would bustle, hustle, and bump into other students with her self-assigned tasks. Students responded with, "Stop, Peley! I'm cooking!" or "It's my turn to iron, now!" Peley would ignore them and proceed with her frantic schedule. The only time she appeared content in the housekeeping center was one day during winter flu season when only she and Jerry were in the center. Peley proceeded to iron, cook, tend the babies, set the table, and serve Jerry. All was accomplished with the precision of an experienced housekeeper and without a word. Clothes were ironed and folded neatly. The baby was gently dressed. The table was carefully set and dinner was fried, stirred, and presented. Jerry sat at the kitchen table, watching intently and, with a smile, finally ate his expertly served meal. Peley seemed to enjoy the role of person in charge of domestic duties; she appeared to perceive this center as serious work.

At home she was the person in charge, since her English was the best in the household. She answered the door and phone and toward the end of the school year, could translate many notes and letters. Even though her grandmother watched over Peley and her brother, Peley was expected to do the physical household chores and take responsibility for getting herself and her brother ready for school in the morning.

Listening Center. This center was equipped with earphones and cassette recorder. Usually a storybook, paper, and art pencils were placed on the round table next to each set of earphones. Children would sit in the chairs and follow along in the books as they listened to stories. Upon completion, they would accomplish an activity related to the story, such as drawing a picture and labeling it with a word or words. Social interactions at this center involved the equipment and group work. If there were problems, they were instructed to help each other before asking for assistance. Students would smile at one another and laugh or sing with the tape. Raji would listen attentively to the story, follow the directions carefully and complete the activity. He enjoyed this center and said, "I like the stories and songs." However, he did not share his enjoyment with the other children at the center with smiles, nods, and sing-a-longs.

On the other hand, Peley would appear to be listening at the center, but would seem to be confused about story activities. She would say in a hushed and hurried voice, "What do we do? I don't like this." No one would respond. She would then copy a neighbor's work quickly and leave the center for the bathroom or drinking fountain. When asked to tell about the center, she pointed to the earphones and responded with, "I don't like this. I don't like them on my ears. They talk fast."

Discovery Center. This center provided a science lesson and reflected the weekly theme related to a nursery rhyme or a letter of the alphabet. Insects, endangered species, germination, and circulatory system were some of the topics tackled. It was a popular place, because of the unusual hands-on opportunities offered the children. A teaching assistant was always on duty to help each group follow the sequentially necessary directions. There was a lot of talk and exchange of ideas among the children at this center. Unfortunately, Peley's social experiences again demonstrated struggles while Raji was intent on his work and didn't interact.

A typical example occurred when eight children were drawing and labeling the daytime sky. Raji drew a rocket ship with what looked like a lunar landing module attached. It was much more intricate than what was typical for this group of children. He focused on his drawing and conversed with no one. Again, Raji's work was ignored.

Instead of Raji's concentration, Peley looked around the table, commented and questioned, "Veronica, you made flowers. They don't go in the sky." Veronica replied, "I like flowers." Then Peley began copying as she observed Linda drawing an arc. Linda exclaimed, "You can't make a rainbow! I am!" Peley quickly turned her arc into what seemed to be a half circle. Linda then asked loudly, "What is?" Peley replied, "I made a rock with a face." Then Veronica and Linda chided, "A rock isn't in the sky!" Peley countered with quiet exasperation, "I don't care!" Linda continued, "I like your sun, Brian." He responded with, "Wow! a rainbow. Look! James made a moon too!"

Block Center. The activities associated with this center's activities took place on the "pretty red rug." Large and small blocks were used to build structures related to the letter or theme for the week. Often step-by-step directions were written on large sheets of construction paper and posted on the side of one of the shelves to explain what was to be accomplished. A teaching assistant would read and elaborate on the instructions to help the students begin the task. Both Peley and Raji encountered social struggles in this center also. Peley would make letters or shapes with the blocks. She would also attempt to talk to members of the group. "I saw you on the bus, Brian. Do you know me?" Brian would shake his head in the positive. Peley would continue, "Do you want to play peek?" She would duck behind a wall of blocks and make loud sounds, "Yuck, Yuck! Heee! Heee!" Sometimes, a student would respond and say, "Peley, don't do that!" At other times they all would ignore her pleas for attention. She would then complain of a pain. "My leg hurts. OOoooh! My leg hurts. I don't feel good. I hurt!" An assistant would come to check on her and ask if she would like to go to the nurse. Peley would reply in the negative and watch the children build.

Later in the year, Peley would put on the construction hard hat and direct the building. "First we have to make the wall and road. The doorway go here for the trucks." Annie, her friend at the time, might listen to her, but the other children would say "No!" or ignore her as they continued construction with a buddy.

When Raji entered the block center, he would immediately begin carrying blocks off the shelf and building. He would hold two large blocks under each arm and say, "Look, I am strong! I am a strong man." No one in the group would comment. He would begin building on his own and then notice a group project. He would attempt to join by adding blocks in various parts of a structure, but soon would be rebuffed. "Don't put it there. It doesn't belong." "No, that's a road." "No, that's a window." "Put your blocks away." Raji would leave the group and build his own creation off to the side of the rug.

Writing/Art Center. This center posed difficulties for Peley and Raji. An example of this occurred one morning while Peley stood at the table and traced her initials from wooden 3" x 6" letters. The other students sat at the table and traced their initials. They were told to decorate the letters with magic markers, glue and glitter. Peley colored her letters with magic marker, looked around at the other children's work, and stated, "I'm done. I don't like this. It stinks! I don't want to do this any more." The other students ignored her and continued to work. They discussed their letters and decorations. "I think I'm using that blue glitter." "I like the silver! Oooooo, this is pretty." "I like yours." Peley chimed in, "My hands are sticky, yuck!" The teaching assistant responded, "Peley, if you are finished, you may go to the art center to draw at the easel." Peley promptly proceeded to the easel and left her initials behind.

At the easel, Peley drew the figure of herself which she repeated in most of her drawings throughout the school year. It was a picture of a tall, lithe woman in a long purple gown covered with crescent moons and stars. The woman had a long black pony tail and green face. Her eyes were black slanted lines and her mouth was a straight red line. Peley stood alone at the easel humming while she attended to her creation.

Raji seemed to work in earnest at the writing center, rarely mixing with the other children. Whenever shaping letters with clay, tracing or decorating letters, he looked neither left nor right. His colors were pinks and purples; he drew delicate flower designs around the letters. Raji's parents explained that this is a typical exercise for school children in India. On several occasions, students asked Raji about his designs. "Why do you put flowers on the letters?" Raji replied, "They look nice there." On another day, a child commented, "Why do you always make flowers? You're being a girly, girly."

A few times during the year he would try to initiate conversation in the group while he was working. "Why is your letter that way?" or "What did you make?" Often there were no responses from the children. On several occasions, the reactions were, "None of your business!" or "We don't like you" or "You make trouble!" Raji would not acknowledge their remarks and continue with his writing task.

When asked what he liked to do best in school, Raji replied, "I like to draw. I like the easel." He was usually so absorbed in the art center or writing center that he was the last to complete the task. He would occasionally create a brown man with obvious muscles in his arms and legs and could be heard murmuring, "This is my muscle man. He is strong." The man would have large eyes and a smile to match.

Math Center. This center was located at a table where children focused on quantitative terms, counting, and number symbols. They used manipulatives while learning sets, shapes, and money. Peley and Raji excelled in the games at the math center. They would learn procedures quickly and be the first to accomplish any task. Socialization again was difficult. Peley would be telling or showing others what to do, "No, it's this way. You make two here. You can't do it!" Raji would finish tasks easily and begin making designs with his manipulatives. While other children attempted to figure out how many acorn piles had more than three in it, Raji would have completed the task and made an acorn picture.

The learning centers appeared to be places where children talked a lot and seemed delighted with the experiences and the people in their groups. Numerous activities were occurring in the classroom at any given moment with group changes made at twenty minute intervals. The negative social interactions experienced by Peley and Raji in the centers were not obvious enough for the teaching assistants and teachers to be overly concerned. Peley and Raji never complained; their classmates rarely reported problems. Occasionally, the teaching assistants and teachers discussed an incident, but because it did not seem to disrupt classroom activities, it was not considered significant.

Additionally, they did not consider the cumulative effect of these incidents, because they were unaware of the frequency and possible causes.

Special Classes

Special classes such as physical education, library, and music provided other perspectives on social interaction. These classes were more traditionally organized with the teacher as leader and students as followers. The teacher controlled the lessons with direct, explicit instructions, thus allowing minimal student interactions. The teacher did most of the talking. But even in these situations, Peley and Raji had difficulties.

Physical education. Once a week, this class was taught by Mrs. Starr in the gymnasium or outdoors. The children played vigorously and enjoyed the running games. Since it was a large group activity structured by the teacher, there were few verbal exchanges among individuals. They cheered, clapped, and screamed as they played relay races, tee ball, tag, soccer, and kick ball. Peley would occasionally become too rough and get hurt. Consequently, she would have to sit out the game or go to the nurse's office. One day, she bumped heads with David while playing tag. On another day, she pushed Raji so hard, he fell and hit his head against the wall. He never cried, but rubbed his head so wildly that Mrs. Starr sent him to the nurse's office.

Raji never became loud or rough in the games. Soccer was his favorite sport. Mrs. Starr made a point of mentioning to the class that Raji knew a lot about the game and was very skilled at maneuvering the ball. But this did not seem to influence the students to include him as they rammed around the soccer field kicking the ball past him.

Music. This class met once a week and was a favorite. The music teacher's lessons were an interesting variety of activities. Whole group involvement was encouraged, so children had little time to talk with each other. The children danced, sang, played musical instruments, heard stories, and expressed their laughter and tears. Nursery rhymes, classical music, children's favorites, and holiday tunes were all part of the program. The music teacher also attempted to coordinate his lessons with the kindergarten program.

At the beginning of the year, Raji and Peley rarely participated during music. They did not know the words to songs and hesitated to volunteer for experimenting with dances or musical instruments. They listened, watched, and mouthed some of the words. By the end of the year, they were laughing, copying body movements, and joyfully learning the words. Peley and Raji often sat next to each other during music class.

Library. Once a week, the children sat on the carpeted library floor while the librarian read a story and led discussions or showed film strips. After the presentation, the children went to one of two library tables where excellent pieces of children's literature had been selected by the librarian. Next, they would study the pictures, words, and stories with a classmate or a small group. Then each child would quickly choose a book to take back to the class.

Peley and Raji did not join with other children during book selections. By January, Peley showed interest in Dr. Seuss books and read them aloud to herself. She would orally read a page, laugh, and then converse noisily with the creatures in the book. Lizbeth also read aloud, but she was usually surrounded by attentive classmates. Raji did not appear to be interested in any of the books on the tables. He would thumb through some of the pages, but rarely attempted to read the story. Unlike most of the children, he couldn't seem to decide on a book to take out of the library. Usually, the teacher helped him with choices, while talking about the books with him.

One winter day, after the librarian showed a film strip of Ezra Jack Keats' award winner, *The Snowy Day*, whose main character is an African American boy, Raji went straight to the librarian and asked to see the book. He stated emphatically, "This is my favorite book! He looks just like me!" Raji had finally found a book he could relate to, simply because the main character resembled him. He chose to take this book home.

Finding Friends

Throughout the year Peley and Raji struggled with social interactions. During December, Peley made many attempts to be friendly with Annie. When given the opportunity to choose someone to work or play, she selected Annie. "Will you be my friend? I want to sit with you. I will call you on the phone. Give me your numbers." Peley tried calling Annie, but copied the nine as a six and was unable to connect. By January, Peley and Annie sat together on the rug. They were placed in centers together and seemed to be inseparable. But the relationship soured when Annie was invited to a classmate's birthday party and Peley was not. When Peley discovered she had not been included, she could not be comforted. She did not hide her tears and anger. When the ESL teacher, Mrs. Brown attempted to reason with her, Peley screamed, "Jeannie took my friend from me!! She took my friend!!" For the rest of the morning, Peley sat with frowning face and arms folded against her chest. She refused to do work and told Mrs. Starr, "I'm sick!" Mrs. Starr allowed her to remain in place to calm herself.

After that incident, Annie would occasionally pair up with Peley, but she chose to be with other friends too. Peley spent most of the rest of the year either alone, in large groups or paired with someone the teacher suggested. By the end of the year, Raji would sit next to Peley or Jerry. "Jerry is my friend. He doesn't say mean things to me." Raji also named Peley in his Kindergarten Yearbook "thank you page" as one of the people who helped him with school. His mother, father, and sister were the other people listed.

Summary of Work and Play

During most of the year, classmate interactions lacked a positive tone for Peley and Raji. Neither child seemed to be able to successfully gain entry into the group. The other children in the class could count on a daily friend, including the child in the class with autistic behaviors.

Peley and Raji sat alone, unable to communicate with classmates at opening ceremonies. Peley was often rude and commanding. Raji kept to himself and made no attempts to engage in conversations. Similarly around the tables in whole group lessons, Peley was critical of neighbors' work while Raji quickly completed tasks and entertained himself. In learning centers, Peley and Raji initiated interactions, but were unsuccessful. Raji would suggest or comment and be immediately rebuffed, left to work alone. Peley would attempt to draw attention to herself or dominate the group effort. The children either ignored, criticized, or confronted her, leaving her turned inward with frown, bent head, and folded arms.

In most special classes, where small group interaction was at a minimum, Peley and Raji struggled. Peley was too rough in physical education classes; Raji's excellent athletic abilities were ignored by the children. Library was a time when Peley read alone and Raji had difficulty finding a book. Neither child was introduced to literature relating to their cultural backgrounds. Few pieces of multicultural literature were available in the school and educators appeared unaware of the purpose or use of the multicultural literature in a literacy program. Mrs. Starr wondered, "We have a wide variety of excellent children's literature in our program, but Peley is only interested in Dr. Seuss books. Raji is rarely able to choose a book without help from one of us." By the end of the year, music class seemed to be the only special class which provided the two children with positive experiences.

Finally, both children did not know consistent friendly social interactions until the end of the school year and that was usually with each other. Raji was confident in asking Peley and Jerry for help and often sat next to them. Peley graciously helped Raji.

Mrs. Starr realized that Peley and Raji had difficulties working and playing with others. She perceived their social and emotional behaviors as the causes of their conflicts and struggles. Terms such as "troubled", "aggressive," and "spoiled" were used to describe Peley. "Shy" and "withdrawn" were the characteristics associated with Raji. Mrs. Starr believed that, in time, Peley and Raji would learn to successfully work and play with the other children in the classroom by simply being involved in the kindergarten program. By the end of the school year, she noted more improvements in their social behaviors, but she was convinced that both children needed summer socialization experiences with other children their age. She recommended that Peley attend day camp and Raji enroll in the summer school literacy program (Schmidt, 1995).

During the school year, it never occurred to Mrs. Starr that the children's struggles might be related to cultural differences between home and school. Even though the home school connection was an important factor in the program, it was not part of Mrs. Starr's experiences or training to consider the importance of the children's cultural differences and their relationship to English literacy learning. The next chapter will describe the components of the kindergarten formal literacy learning program and the children's progress in each.

Peley and Raji were taken from the classroom community to participate in the ESL program which was not coordinated with the classroom literacy program.

4

Conflict and Struggle: Literacy Learning Program

The kindergarten formal literacy learning program for Peley and Raji contained three basic components: learning centers and teacher-developed activities, a literature-based reading program with ESL pull-out classes and a language component with computer-assisted instruction.

Similar to Clay's study of bilingual children's parental support (1971), Peley's and Raji's parents encouraged English literacy learning at home. Peley was responsible for answering the telephone and by the end of the school year could translate many notes and letters from school. She also proudly read Doctor Seuss books to her mother. Nightly, Raji's parents worked with him as he studied numbers and letters and learned sight words with flash cards. Nevertheless, the children's English literacy learning in school was marked with struggle. Their experiences were consistent with the literature on language-minority literacy development (Swain, 1972; Au & Mason, 1981; Fishman, 1989; Trueba, et al., 1990). When the school program ignores or rarely makes cultural connections between home and school, cultural conflict and struggle become apparent.

The children's English literacy development varied in this kindergarten program. In order to understand their progress, the background and detailed descriptions of each component of the program will be presented along with dialogue and scenes from actual literacy lessons (Schmidt 1993a, 1993b).

Background of the Formal Literacy Program

Several years ago, the kindergarten educators at East Side Elementary School realized that their children were having difficulties in the formal literacy program. The kindergarten screening tests which took place in July revealed that the children did not seem to possess the experiences necessary to become successful readers and writers in the primary grades. Some children could not recognize letters in the alphabet and knew little about grapheme-phoneme connections. The educators suspected that school-related literacy activities rarely occurred in the homes. Therefore, the children might have been deprived of thousands of hours necessary for preparation in beginning reading (Chomsky, 1972; Heath, 1983). The data demonstrated a need for change; the concepts for their new literacy program were born.

During the next five years, the team of tenured kindergarten teachers with less than ten years teaching experience, the preschool teaching assistant, and the computer teaching assistant worked collaboratively to create and develop the three basic components of the program: teacher-developed activities and educational learning centers (Fein, 1975; Vandenberg, 1981; Gump, 1989), *World of Reading Series* (Pearson, Johnson, Clymer, Indrisano, Venezky, Baumann, Hiebert, & Toth, 1991), a literature-based reading program and a language component with *IBM Writing-To-Read* (Martin,1984), a computer-assisted program. All three emphasized direct instruction in phonological awareness (Ball & Blachman, 1991), basic print awareness (Holdaway, 1979; Clay, 1972), word awareness, (Ehri, 1976) and letter recognition (Chall, 1967; Bond & Dykstra, 1967). All were considered necessary for beginning literacy activities in the school setting.

Teaching perspectives in this kindergarten ranged from mastery of specific skills to holistic language learning (Leu & Kinzer, 1986). Some lessons stressed comprehension, while others stressed the skills for word recognition. Direct explicit instruction as well as indirect discovery methods were used. There appeared to be no pure top-down or bottom-up perspective, since the teachers in this program saw reading as a complex process.

Another important feature of this kindergarten was the early childhood education program. Four female high school students spent the morning working as teacher aides in the three kindergarten classrooms. In the afternoons, they studied academics at the high school. The young women were trained and supervised by kindergarten teachers and the preschool teaching assistant. They helped in lesson preparation, gave children individualized attention, and served as the extra pairs of hands needed to put the kindergarten literacy program into practice.

Learning Centers and Teacher-Developed Activities

The kindergarten teachers created learning centers as settings for literacy learning which would systematically integrate reading, writing, listening, and speaking within the total kindergarten classroom schedule (Teale, 1982). They did not want to limit literacy learning to specific times associated with the formal literature-based and computer-assisted programs. Therefore, they integrated curriculum ideas and learning opportunities for a specific subject into educational learning centers. Centers actually provided the means for literacy learning as children socialized and communicated. Basic concepts in a hands-on, discovery-oriented environment promoted student interactions. Children worked independently and in small groups, with teacher as facilitator (Kantor, et al.,1992; Neuman & Roskos, 1992). In this role, teachers believed that they would have time to observe and record individual learning process and progress for needs assessment and evaluation. The kindergarten educators hoped this literate environment would help to allieviate the years of suspected, neglected literacy activities.

Learning Centers

During the first week of school, printed labels on objects appeared everywhere in the classroom for letter and word recognition. Words were pronounced and letter-sound connections repeated. The labeled items included "clock," "chair," "table," and "door,"and children's names were posted on the learning center board for the daily center assignments. At the beginning of the school year, before reading groups were formed, educational learning center activities took place during the first forty minutes of the day as the first vehicles for literacy learning. There were nine centers in three classrooms, and children went to a different one each day with a group of children selected from the three classrooms. The activities in each center related to a weekly theme, such as a letter of the alphabet or a nursery rhyme.

When Humpty Dumpty was the theme, students listened to the rhyme and circled words in the listening center, followed Humpty Dumpty sequential instructions in the block center, traced ovals and labeled them in the writing center, examined actual goose, duck, and chicken eggs in the discovery center, prepared eggs for breakfast in the housekeeping center, put together Humpty Dumpty puzzles in the readiness center, decorated eggs in the art center, studied the concept of one dozen in the math center, and built Humpty Dumpty sand walls with colorful plastic eggs in the sand and water center.

Peley and Raji easily completed activities in the centers, but they rarely had positive social experiences. They were usually ignored or admonished by the other children when they made attempts to communicate.

Peley openly preferred the block center and housekeeping center where she appeared to dramatize stories. Even while at other centers, she would have an eye turned to the action in those centers. At the block center, she would create great roads and bridges. "Look, this bridge goes over the river. It's far, very far!" Members of the group wouldn't respond. In the housekeeping center, she would immediately take over the kitchen, moving around and talking rapidly to herself. "Where are the dishes? I am the cook. I can make food to eat. It will be very very good!" The children would try to stay out of her way.

At the block center, Raji would attempt to share in the building, but was usually pushed away. When the group was designing a castle, he decided to contribute a block with a pointed arch for the entrance. He was quickly dismissed with, "That doesn't go there! Put it away!" Raji moved back and while alone, began erecting a tower of blocks.

Raji also enjoyed the writing/art center. He would play with the clay and tell what he was making to anyone who asked. "I am making letters. You can make letters for words." From clay, he shaped letters into an "S", "R", "T"or "M". Painting was another favorite. He designed intricate flowers in pinks and purples, typical creations for school children in India. He also enjoyed drawing brown, muscle men with smiles. By the end of the year, Raji was no longer designing the flowers since students had openly mocked him for his creations. His muscle man lost the smile and became expressionless.

Teacher-Developed Activities

Opening ceremonies. Opening ceremonies came after learning centers in the fall kindergarten schedule. From the beginning, phonological awareness and syllabication was a daily occurrence. Mrs. Starr took attendance by clapping the syllables of each student's first name. The class mimicked, and then the child proceeded alone. If a child had difficulty coordinating the word parts with speech, Mrs. Starr guided the clapping and repetition. She encouraged listening and saying segments of familiar names and words, especially those with rhyming sounds, along with calendar names, dates, and birthdays. Next, the weather was described by one of the children standing by a window. The children chanted and clapped, "Weatherman, weatherman, what do you say, what kind of weather do we have today?" Pictures representing the words "cloudy," "sunny," or "rainy," etc. were placed on the calendar, and the clapping continued for weather words. Finally, The Pledge of Allegiance was recited as one child held the flag; by November most children had memorized it.

Peley and Raji usually sat alone during the daily opening procedures. They followed along easily and were able to successfully recite, pronounce, and recognize letters, sounds, words, and numbers. However, Raji rarely volunteered for classroom tasks or answers.   By the end of the year, Peley was offering responses to questions and asking to be chosen. Her hand would shoot up in the air to give an answer or beg for selection.

Rotating lessons. Rotating language, math, fine motor, and gross motor lessons were next on the day's schedule. Stories and poems read by the teachers provided themes for attentive listening, class discussions, field trips, language experience stories and development of fine and gross motor coordination.   For instance, if *S* was the letter of the week, the spider in the "Little Miss Muffet" rhyme would be the focus. "Little Miss Muffet" dramatics would occur. Spiders would be studied in the discovery center and pipe cleaner spiders made in the art center. Clay *S*s, cut out *S*s, painted *S*s and so on would be formed in the writing center and rubber spider sets manipulated during math lessons. The children would be taught a spider song that included hand and body motions for practice in coordination.

Peley and Raji learned the "Itsy Bitsy Spider" song quickly and followed the movements, but their responses were different. The following scene from "Itsy Bitsy Spider" demonstrates their reactions:

The teacher paired the children and directed one child's hands as the spider and the other child's back as the water spout. Peley's partner was Jennifer, a slight, blond-haired child. Peley had often tried to sit near her in class, but Jennifer consistently thwarted Peley's attempts. When Jennifer's spider movements began on Peley's back, Peley became irritated. She squirmed and wriggled and said, "I don't like this. I don't like it!" When it was Peley's turn to be the spider, she roughly poked and pushed on Jennifer's back. Mrs. Starr came to the rescue, "Be a gentle spider, Peley. Spiders are quiet and careful."

When Jennifer again gently moved her fingers up Peley's back, Peley yelled, "Stop!" Mrs. Starr quietly stated, "Peley, you may sit down on the rug if you like." Peley sat alone with her head bent to her knees while Jennifer stood and watched the others.

On the other hand, Raji was gentle and seemed to understand that this was a game of slow, careful movements. He and his partner, Jamey, an unusually active child, concentrated, taking turns being spiders. Their spiders earned praises from Mrs. Starr. This was one of Raji's few obvious positive moments during the school year.

Sharing Time. Sharing time provided opportunites for oral language development. This was a daily occurrence on the large brown rug next to the blackboard. Children brought in homework and objects to share from home and placed them in a plastic basket under the blackboard. Mrs. Starr was seated in a chair next to the basket, where she modeled appropriate comments and questions for the students seated cross-legged on the rug. She would take an object from the basket and ask the owner to come forward to share. She would also encourage audience participation in the form of questions and comments. At first, the children presenting and questioning were shy, but by the end of the year, paticipation was enthusiastic.

In the beginning of the year, Peley brought in a plastic harmonica and leaned on Mrs. Starr, refusing to speak. By the end of the year, she would explain a drawing or piece of writing from her school work, but she brought nothing from home. Raji, however, was the only child who did not share throughout the school year.

Snack time. Snack time was an interlude for quiet conversation. Children brought in crackers and cookies to share with the rest of the class. In the beginning of the year, both Peley and Raji seldom tasted the commercial snacks. By the end of the year, they were both trying the assortment of chocolate-coated and sugar-filled cookies. During May, in a class discussion about favorite foods, Peley stated what most other children had chosen: "Pizza is my favorite food." When Raji claimed his favorite, "I like pears and rice," classmates reacted with disgust, "Terrible!"or "Yuck!"or "I don't get it!"

Reading aloud. Mrs. Starr, the high school aides, or the teaching assistant read stories aloud as part of the daily schedule. They hoped to develop print awareness as well as to model literate activity. A short discussion with cutting, pasting, or drawing activities reinforced the story, which usually was coordinated with the letter theme for the week. The letter appeared on the blackboard each Monday in its upper and lower case forms with a poem nearby using illiteration. Choral reading of the poem occurred daily. Children also printed the letter and drew pictures associated with the letter in their teacher-created alphabet books. Peley and Raji easily completed this weekly assignment. During read-alouds, it was discovered that idiomatic expressions were problematic for Peley and Raji. "Sly as a fox," "easy as pie," and "strong as an ox" could be completed orally by most children, when the last word of the phrase was omitted. Mrs. Starr would say, "Smart as an____" and children would raise their hands and yell, "owl!" Peley and Raji were visibly confused by these exercises. Peley eyed other students and looked around as if lost. Raji frowned and kept his eyes straight ahead. Neither child attempted answers. When called upon, they gave no responses.

Beginning Formal Reading and Language Instruction

At the end of two months of lesson rotation among the three kindergarten classrooms, the three teachers evaluated children's progress and readiness to begin formal reading and language instruction. Three ability groups were formed based on recognition of the alphabet, grapheme-phoneme connections, fine and gross motor coordination, and teachers' judgements of class participation. Several students were moved into and out of classes to accomodate two ability groups in each room. This appeared to cause no problems since the children had become familiar with teachers, classrooms, and classmates while participating in all nine learning centers.

Mrs. Starr had sixteen students in the top reading group for the entire kindergarten. Included in the top group was a child with autistic behaviors, assisted by a teacher aide and a communication board (Duncan, 1996). Peley and Raji were also in the top group. Additionally, Mrs. Starr took another group of five children considered academically average. The other two kindergarten classes had low and average groups only.

When reading groups were formed, learning center time was decreased to twenty minutes per morning in order to make time for the formal reading program and language components of the literacy program.

Literature-Based Reading Series

The second component of this kindergarten literacy program was a literature-based reading series which provided a framework for formal reading instruction. The teachers in the school district chose *World of Reading Series* (Pearson, et al.,1991) after studying several other series and viewing presentations from publishing companies. Additionally, the teachers opted to receive in-service training during the summer and first school year, so they would learn to adapt the series to the needs of their children.

Series description and use. *World of Reading Series* (1991) was written from an interactive perspective advocating the teaching of reading skills in context. Similar to the teacher-created component of the kindergarten literacy program, the reading lessons encouraged listening to stories and learning letter-sound correspondence for phonological awareness. Word awareness and letter recognition were explicitly taught through practice with oral language, experience with words in books, and recognition of word labels in the classroom environment.

Big Shared Books with predictable stories and nursery rhymes permitted greater teacher/student interactions and group participation. The teacher read the book and tracked the print as children echo-read and took turns tracking the print. Wordless books also added opportunities for experimentation in oral language and study of sequence in story retellings. Teaching students that reading has meaning and purpose was encouraged in this kindergarten through inferential questioning and class discussions.

The series used thematic, integrated language arts units to teach skills in context. Early lessons concentrated on name recognition, knowing colors, understanding shapes and directions, identifying numerals 1-10, and reciting address, phone number, and days of the week. In the first kindergarten book, Mother Goose rhymes were read and recited for emphasis on phonological awareness and grapheme-phoneme connections. The second kindergarten book had versions of fairy tales such as "The Little Red Hen and the Fox;" many were composed with rhyming words. Sixteen words were introduced in the book, and word recognition cards and games promoted vocabulary learning. The top group in Mrs. Starr's classroom skipped the readiness portion and began the second kindergarten book. They finished the first two preprimers by June. At the same time, the average group completed the readiness and the kindergarten portion of the series.

Ability grouping was important in this school district, as well as in East Side elementary's kindergarten program, even though it was discouraged in the literature-based series. However, reciprocal teaching, peer tutoring, and independent and cooperative learning were typical practices in the top group.

Assessment was another important element of the series. The teachers were instructed about the value of listening and observing children. Verbal student reports, anecdotal records, interviews, conferences, portfolio assessments, and observational checklists were used. Formal testing included placement tests and unit process tests. Comprehension was checked when students read passages and responded to open-ended questions. Skills tests were administered at midbook and end-of-book. Mrs. Starr valued "kid watching"(Goodman, 1986) procedures and the skill tests, but the building reading teacher interpreted test results and took charge of the end of the year formal testing, evaluation and placement.

There was a multicultural strand of literature offered in the series, but this strand was not used by the ESL or kindergarten programs. Teachers believed it was not needed for literacy learning.

Workbooks were considered valuable, because they were coordinated with each story for word recognition, phonological awareness and reading-writing connections. Readers' journals, videos, classroom libraries, toys associated with stories, such as puppets or miniature objects, were added for interest. Teacher resource kits with charts and posters, big book and little book kits, and assessment kits were other features which aided the learning process. Additionally, examples of home/school correspondence demonstrated the ways and means for parents to model literacy with reading and writing activities.

For the most part, Mrs. Starr enjoyed the literature-based series. She saw it as a component of the literacy program which motivated learning to read and taught the necessary skills. However, she found the series demanding for half-day kindergarten, since it was difficult to accomplish the daily lessons in twenty minutes.

The Top Reading Group

Reading lessons were presented to the top group on the big brown rug. Mrs. Starr was seated in a chair with the blackboard on her left and a reading chart standing on her right. A shelf under the blackboard held eraserless pencils in a coffee can and wooden framed black slates. The children sat cross-legged, in rows or a semicircle on the rug and held slates on their laps as surfaces for writing answers in their workbooks. The pencils without erasers served to remind children that the process of making errors is a natural part of learning.

A story in the reading group could take several days to complete. The lesson might begin with an introduction to vocabulary and teacher explanation of a reading skill. Vocabulary or skill exercises in a workbook or worksheet would follow. Next, Mrs. Starr would begin questioning for prior knowledge using pictures from the literature. The children's animated discussions would lead to the the reading and exploration of ideas around sentences and new vocabulary. Finally, Mrs. Starr would read aloud a big book, an oversized version of the children's books and point to pictures and words. The children would follow along, keeping all eyes forward. At the end of the story, they would review the pages, taking turns pointing to words and sentences while choral reading. Finally, miniature replicas of the big book would be distributed to the children for silent reading and partner read-alouds.

Sequence. Peley and Raji were placed in the top reading group, consisting of sixteen children, but left the group two times a week for their ESL pull-out program. Since several consecutive days were necessary to study one story, the two children appeared continually confused during reading group. They frequently lost their places in practice exercises and couldn't follow the teacher's oral directions. This was first evidenced by their problems with sequencing exercises that took place the day after the children read a story.

Mrs. Starr would begin to reread the story and stop after a few sentences. The students were expected to circle what came next on a worksheet with four pictures. Raji would seem to be paying attention by watching the teacher as she read. Peley would seem not to attend to the reading, but would fiddle with her socks or look away appearing to be in another world. If they circled a choice, it would occur after glimpsing a neighbor's sheet or asking a neighbor for help. The other group members easily accomplished these activities, so Peley's and Raji's behaviors were different.

A reading lesson in March was a specific example of sequence confusion. Mrs. Starr began the lesson, "What is the first thing you do in the morning?" Children in the class began volunteering. After several answers, Peley and Raji were called upon. Peley looked away from Mrs. Starr. Raji stared at Mrs. Starr and said, "I don't know."

Mrs. Starr continued the lesson by introducing puzzles of routine sequential tasks, such as a postman delivering mail, Asian American and African American children caring for their pets, and adults accomplishing household chores. She explained, "We will work with a buddy and look at these puzzle pieces. Let's put them together to show what happened, first, second, third and last."

On this rare occasion, Raji and Peley were paired. They immediately took the pieces in hand and studied the shapes of the puzzles from differing angles. Without speaking to each other, they completed the puzzles without looking at the pictures. Since the puzzles could only fit together one way, sequence was not a consideration. Mrs. Starr checked their work and congratulated, "You showed the first thing that happened, the second thing that happened and the last thing that happened. Great!"

Vocabulary activities. Workbook pages dealing with vocabulary were completed as a whole group on the rug while Mrs. Starr overlooked from her chair. Answers that involved filling in the blanks or circling the pictures would be checked immediately. Peley and Raji seemed to have difficulties figuring out what to do on each page. Sometimes they would ask for help, but usually they ignored the pages or copied answers from someone.

Vocabulary activities in the workbook were always connected to a story. Mrs. Starr would say a word representing an object and the kindergarten students would circle the object in a picture found on a workbook page. Peley and Raji easily identified and circled words such as *dish, sun,* and *dog,* but they became visibly agitated one day when they couldn't find *dot* and *bun*. The *dot* was on a bedspread and the *bun* was a hamburger bun. They knew neither and Peley frantically asked, "What is it? I don't know!" When she was shown the correct answers, Raji watched and circled his.

Matching beginning sounds in word-picture associations also seemed difficult for Peley and Raji. During one lesson, they could not understand pictures of *game, yard, garden, vest, box, bag, vine,* and *bird*. Peley would say, "I don't know this. What's this?" Then she would skip the pages flipping past them quickly. When she found a page she seemed to understand, she would say, "Good!" and finish it quickly and correctly. Raji would stare at a page and then close the book. He would sit quietly and wait until most students had completed the work and the teacher had given instructions for the next part of the day. Then, he'd put his book away unfinished.

A small segment of a vocabulary lesson in April indicated that Raji continued to be confused about certain English vocabulary.

Mrs. Starr:	Today we are going to read from our story books, but first we must look at the words we need to know. The words are *get, it, ride,* and *help*. We will read each word in a sentence on the chart and then make a sentence to go with it. Peley, will you read the first one?
Peley:	We get a ride.
Mrs. Starr:	Yes, Peley! Now can you make a sentence?
Peley:	Get the pencil.
Mrs. Starr:	Very good. Get a pencil. Now Raji, can you make a sentence?
Raji:	Ride a baby.

[Mrs. Starr squinted as if puzzled by Raji's answer. She then called on Jerry.]

Jerry:	We get a ride to school.
Mrs. Starr:	Yes, Jerry! We get a ride to school.

Silent reading and reading aloud. Stories read silently with a buddy posed problems for Peley and Raji. Mrs. Starr explained silent reading, "First, read the words inside your head. Then, take turns and read aloud to your buddy." Children were encouraged to pair up during that time. Peley would ask one of the girls to pair with her, but she was usually told, "No, I am with Linda" or "No, I am with Jennifer." Once, when Mrs. Starr paired Peley with Nanci, the tiny, blond, curly-haired child broke into tears, claiming to need the nurse for her headache. Nanci was allowed to leave the room, but returned in perfect health at the end of reading time.

By February, Peley was reading Doctor Seuss books. She would go off by herself when free time was available and read silently or aloud in the reading corner. None of the students seemed to pay attention to her accomplishment. Mrs. Starr noticed and began giving regular praise. This may have accounted for Jennifer's loud request for Peley as a reading partner in March. Peley and Jennifer sat together as Mrs. Starr instructed the children in the group, "Read inside your heads, and then read to each other. You can be teachers. Point to the words and read your books to each other. When you are finished, you may go to your learning center."

This activity with the little predictable books was a review for the children. They had memorized a lot of the words such as, *I, can, look, play, Boris, Morris, playground,* and *children,* but were stumbling on words such as, *said, yelled, out, went, want, girl, through, swings,* and *monkey.* However, the books actually seemed too difficult for them since their attempts at saying the words proved frustrating. Several children abruptly dropped their books and went to centers. Peley and Jennifer focused on the pictures and beginning sounds, but were unable to figure out much of the book, *Morris and Boris at the Playground.* Jennifer soon gave up and went to the book corner to read. Peley persisted, but eventually followed Jennifer.

Raji usually read alone, but toward the end of the year, he gravitated toward Jerry or Peley for partner reading.

Wondering. During the last months of school, Mrs. Starr began teaching the children about "wondering" as a prediction exercise. In one lesson, the children were told to think of "I wonder" questions when they read silently in their heads. Mrs. Starr went around the room and asked each student what they were wondering as they were reading.

Peley:	I wonder what will happen to dog.
Linda:	I wonder about the cat.
Jeff:	I wonder about the hen.
Raji:	I don't know.
Mrs. Starr:	Vicki, what do you wonder?
Vicki:	I wonder about the dog's bone?
Jerry:	I wonder about the end?

Mrs. Starr: Raji, do you wonder about anything in the story?

Raji: I don't know.

Raji didn't seem to understand this activity.

Riddles. Finally, a reading lesson in May demonstrated Raji's and Peley's continuous struggles during reading group. A riddle was printed on primary paper introducing the reading lesson.

Mrs. Starr: A riddle is like a poem and as you read it, you guess what it's talking about. By the end of the riddle, you will guess. I will read the riddle and then you guess what it is talking about.

> Bugs, bugs listen to me.
> I have a riddle for you.
> Forgive me, but listen carefully
> To my one and only clue.
> I am sticky, I am icky.
> Put your foot on me and feel.
> Aha! you're caught in me.
> A sweet and tasty spider's meal.
> What am I?

The students did not attempt to guess. A few hands were raised, but when called upon, the students had no answers.

Mrs. Starr: I'll read it again and you listen and raise your hands when you know the answer.

When she finished reading, most hands went up including Raji's.

Mrs. Starr: Raji, what is it?

Raji: Boy.

Mrs. Starr: Vicki, what is it?

Vicki: Spider web.

Mrs. Starr: Right, where could a spider build a web?

Students offered many places, such as, *corners, trees, outside, inside, in the garage, in the cellar*. Peley and Raji did not volunteer answers.

Mrs. Starr: Now we are going to read a story about a spider and think about "I wonder" questions. You know "I wonder" questions. We've done them before. I will read the story in your book today and you will read it tomorrow. The name of the story is the "Big Surprise." I wonder what it is about?

[Mrs. Starr showed the first pages].

Children:	[Chimed in as a chorus] A spider!
Mrs. Starr:	Let's ask "I wonder" questions.
Joe:	I wonder if he'll make a spider web?
Betty:	I wonder where is the web?
Vicki:	I wonder what it will look like?
Jerry:	I wonder what will happen to it?
Mrs. Starr:	Use your imaginations while I read.

After reading the story Mrs. Starr continued her questions.

Mrs. Starr:	What was the big surprise?
Nanci:	The man takes the umbrella.
Mrs. Starr:	Why was the umbrella not a good place for the web?
Annie:	It rained. The man took the umbrella
Mrs. Starr:	Where is a better place for a spider web?
Jimmy:	The wheel!
Mrs. Starr:	Why is the wheel a better place than the umbrella?
Linda:	He won't take it. The wheel stays there.
Mrs. Starr:	Yes! Tomorrow we will read the story together. Some of you will be able to read certain parts. Someone will be the dog; someone will be the spider; someone will be the cat and someone will be the narrator, the person who reads the story.

The students in this reading group lesson participated by answering questions, nodding, raising hands, and watching the teacher. They seemed involved as a group. However, Peley, sat in the back of the group playing with a little bottle of perfume from home. She rolled it in her hands and opened and closed the cap. Raji never offered another answer or raised his hand after the first attempt, but he sat near the teacher and seemed to be listening intently.

Peley and Raji missed the lesson on riddles that had preceded this one, because of attendance in their ESL classes. Descriptions and transcriptions of several ESL sessions demonstrate how unrelated they were to the kindergarten literacy program.

ESL Program

Mrs. Brown, the ESL teacher, was considered an important member of the literacy program for Peley and Raji. She was a slightly built woman, in her early thirties, with short, softly curled, blonde-brown hair, a gentle voice and a sweet smile. She took the children from reading group twice a week to work on grapheme-phoneme connections and oral language development. Mrs. Brown read stories and promoted conversation through discussions of holidays, letter-sound, and word games and a variety of visuals and toys. She believed the students needed time away from the classroom to experiment with oral language. There was no planned coordination between the kindergarten classroom and ESL lessons.

In the fall, Peley resisted leaving the kindergarten classroom. When Mrs. Brown appeared and softly called her by the kindergarten door, Peley would catch a glimpse and not budge. This forced Mrs. Brown to enter the classroom. She would quietly approach Peley who was seated on the rug or at a table and find her hand, "We're going to play a fun game today. We're going to read a story. You'll like it." Peley would keep her head down and respond unequivocally, "I don't want to go." With more coaxing, the child would be led slowly to the door. Finally, in the hallway, Peley would escape Mrs. Brown's hand and race ahead. She would ignore the calls and end up on the second floor of the building in the tiny ESL room seated in Mrs. Brown's chair.

On the other hand, Raji would show no expression when Mrs. Brown came for him and Peley. He would see her, get up, and follow along, quietly observing Mrs. Brown's preoccupation with Peley's run down the hallways.

The ESL room had been a second floor office for a school administrator of yesteryear. It was a small, rectangular-shaped setting, lined with dark, wooden built-in cabinets and bookshelves. A few children's books and word and letter games were on the shelves. One formica-covered round table with five chairs around it was crowded in the middle of the room. The teacher's chair was behind the table and pushed against a bulletin board with a world map stapled on it.

The following is an excerpt from a typical ESL class in the fall of the school year. When Mrs. Brown and Raji arrived in the room, Peley sat with an authoritative demeanor in the teacher's chair.

Mrs. Brown: Peley, you are the teacher!
[Peley beamed, dashed out of the seat, went to the shelf and retrieved a vowel game]

Peley:	We are playing the game today!
Mrs. Brown:	[Firmly] No, Peley, only on Thursday. Today is Tuesday.
Peley:	Last time you say we play a game!
Mrs. Brown:	[Firmly] No, Peley, I said we would play letter games on Thursday and today is Tuesday. We are going to play a story game. Come and sit at the table. I have some pictures to show you.

[Peley came back to the table and half crawled and sprawled over the top of it, blocking Raji's view of the pictures.]

Mrs. Brown:	[Calmly] Peley, sit down in the chair, so we can see the picture together.

[Mrs. Brown showed 9" x 12" laminated pictures in shades of brown, cream, and yellow tones depicting various health services and types of illness. There were children and adults in the pictures who were People of Color and White.]

Mrs. Brown:	Choose any card you like and tell a story about the card.

[Peley chose an Asian boy sitting in a dentist chair. Raji chose a Caucasian boy being weighed and measured by a female African American nurse.]

Mrs. Brown:	Raji, What is the boy doing in the picture?
Raji:	The boy is weigh.
Mrs. Brown:	Who is weighing him?
Raji:	The doctor.
Mrs. Brown:	That's close. The *nurse* is weighing him.

[Meanwhile Peley began crawling on the table and under the table and making sounds, "Yuk! Yuk! Yuk!"]

Mrs. Brown:	[Exasperated] Peley, please pay attention. Tell us about your picture.
Peley:	I don't know. I don't like this. I want to draw on the board. I don't like those pictures.
Mrs. Brown:	[With resignation] Okay. You all may draw on the board.

Peley, with chalk in hand began carefully sketching what she claimed to be a self-portrait. It was a woman in a long-sleeved, full-length gown. She wore a large bow in her long pony tail and her face included slanted lines for eyes and one straight line for a mouth.

Raji, also wrote a huge "R" on the chalkboard. It had a smiling face in the circular upper portion of the letter. Next to it, he drew a long cylindrical object that resembled a musical instrument with about twelve key holes running lengthwise.

Mrs. Brown:	Tell me about your picture, Raji.

[Raji turned around and looked at her, but did not respond.]

Mrs. Brown:	[Pointing to the musical instrument] Raji tell me about

that.
[Again, he turned around and looked at her and then turned to the drawing. He finally responded while facing the blackboard.]
     Raji: I don't know.
[Peley began copying Raji's drawing.]
     Peley: Look at mine. Yuk! Yuk!

Mrs. Brown looked at her watch and informed the children that they could go back to class. Peley bounded out; Raji quickly followed. Neither child looked at the teacher or spoke farewells.

Soon after this lesson, Mrs. Brown decided to see Peley and Raji separately, since she believed Peley dominated the class. Consequently, Peley began demonstrating an even greater resistance to being pulled out of class. She became belligerent crying out, "I won't go!" Finally, on one of the days she was especially tearful, Mrs. Starr took her aside and explained, "Peley, you need to go. This class will help you with your reading and writing. It is important for you. Sometimes, we will let you choose a friend to go."

From that day on, Peley rarely resisted attending ESL class. She usually left during reading or a special project. The only hint of dissatisfaction was her instant frown, but she never called out or cried again.On the occasions when she was allowed to choose a friend, she selected Annie; Annie smiled at the chance for a change of scene.

Raji went to India in December and January of the school year. When he returned, Mrs. Brown attempted to place Peley and Raji together again. Peley saw Raji as a returning friend. However, both children's faces often revealed grim expressions when pulled out of class. Peley would grasp Raji's hand, and seriously take charge of their leave.

The Language Program
The third component or language component, as Mrs. Starr called it, divided the kindergarten class into top and average ability groups. The children in these groups were the same as those in the literature-based top and average reading groups. The top group of sixteen students was placed in the computer-assisted writing-to-read lab during the same time as first grade students labeled "at risk."

The five students in the average group were not considered

ready for the computer lab and received their instruction in the kindergarten classroom from the teaching assistant while the top group went to the computer lab. The average group lessons were planned collaboratively by the kindergarten teacher and the teaching assistant. Early in the year, their lessons were based on read-alouds followed by language activities, such as drawing and labeling pictures. Later in the year, they wrote one or two sentences about a picture or story, using invented spelling. They shared their stories with the whole class when the top group returned from the writing-to-read lab.

Writing-To-Read

The *IBM Writing-To-Read* (Martin, 1984) computer-assisted program, located upstairs from the kindergarten classroom, was a highly structured learning center with technological equipment and language arts materials. Mrs. Starr, acting as a teacher-leader, was trained during summer workshops along with other interested staff before and after the program was initiated in the school.

A teaching assistant, Mrs. Gerard, was hired to take charge of the form and function of the program. She was a vivacious woman in her thirties with light brown, shoulder length, permed hair. Wearing the latest style clothing seen in teen magazines, hot oranges, pinks and greens dominated her stirrup pants and oversized sweaters. Mrs. Gerard emanated light and energy as she spoke with breathless expression and translated her zest to the learning lab and its equipment. She created schedules and materials, maintained the children's progress charts, and supervised the kindergarten and first grade teachers who served as assistants in the lab. Her plans were approved by the classroom teachers, but showed little coordination with classroom themes. Mrs. Gerard read aloud to the children at least once a week using the flannel board for teaching sequence. The children were often allowed to play with the flannel board in order to practice sequence and the retelling of a story.

The top group came to the writing-to-read lab when reading groups were formed in November. Mrs. Starr acted as an assistant during the forty minutes, giving individual and group help and listening to stories. Students usually were assigned two of the seven stations daily. At the stations, they began naming and recognizing letters in uppercase and lower case, making letters out of clay, tracing letters in a tracing tray, writing letters on chalkboard and in an activity book, finding and typing letters on a keyboard, seeing letters that go together to make words and seeing word parts in whole words. They worked in pairs at most of the stations to promote cooperative learning.

Students became experts in computer word processing and other programs. The teachers believed that these activities helped children take control of their own learning. The computer programs, as well as other stations, entitled, *Silly Sentences, Make Words* games, and *Work Journal*, taught principles and patterns in word-making and provided opportunities for writing sentences and stories. Also, the consistent phonemic spelling system presented 42 phonemes to teach students that speech sounds can be written. The phonemes were divided into ten instructional cycles. Each cycle introduced three cycle words that used a set of phonemes. For example, *cat, dog,* and *fish* were studied in terms of the phonemes *a, c, d, f, g, i, o, t* and *sh*. As students combined phonemes, they saw and heard words and recognized spelling patterns. For instance, the computer showed a picture of a cat and the word *cat* appeared under it. Then the computer voice said, "Cat." Next, the children typed *cat* and said "Cat." Finally, *cat* and similar *at* words were written in the work journals.

Seven stations in the writing-to-read lab served seven specific functions. Each station will be described along with the behaviors usually exhibited by Peley and Raji.

Computer Station. The first station or computer station consisted of computers equipped with earphones and special instructional programs designed to teach grapheme-phoneme connections. Students interacted with the programs when a voice told them to say sounds to make a word. They were asked to tap, clap, and type sounds; word patterns followed.

Typically, Peley was paired with Ashton, an African American child, who had difficulty making grapheme-phoneme connections. Early in the program, Mrs. Gerard explained that this was not the best way for Ashton to learn to read and write, but his father had insisted that Ashton be involved in the program.

Frequently, Peley would become impatient while listening to the sounds and words transmitted on the earphones and lose interest. She knew the answers easily, and would type them correctly and quickly. Then, she would look away with a frown on her face and rarely respond to the earphone voice. Meanwhile, Ashton would struggle along, attempting to do the work. He would tell Peley, "Pay attention. You're not doing this. We have to do this! Wait for me!" Mrs. Gerard would hear Ashton and scold Peley. "You must pay attention to your work, Peley. Let me hear you clap and say the sounds for *el! ee! gee! l-e-g!* You need practice and you can help Ashton." Peley would follow Mrs. Gerard's instructions for a short time, but then look to other stations.

Raji would work alone at the station, following the exercises, carefully clapping and repeating the letters and sounds heard. For example, when asked about the word he was typing at a practice session, he pronounced, "Sad", slowly enunciating each sound. When asked what the word meant, he quickly stated, "It's a feeling." When asked if he liked working at the computers, he responded, "I don't like this. I don't like the loud sounds." When the earphones were checked, the volume often would be too loud. Mrs. Gerard would turn it down, but in the process, add that Raji must learn to attend to the work at the station. He frequently left the station for the bathroom or a drink.

Work Journal Station. The work journal station, with earphones and cassettes, reinforced what was learned in the computer station. Students wrote sounds and words using pens and crayons; erasure was discouraged to encourage student risk taking since making errors was considered a necessary learning experience. Peley would sit with Ashton, insert the tape in the recorder and put on the earphones. She would open her work journal and begin writing, not bothering to wait for the tape's directions. A typical example of this occurred when the Sun Tape lesson was studied. Peley and Ashton were required to listen to the tape and follow directions for completing the work journal. The tape gave them directions to make and write the *s* sound, then the *u* sound and finally, the *n* sound. Last, they were required to match the word to the picture of a sun. Ashton said the picture was a mirror and drew a line between the word, *sun* and *mirror*. Peley ignored him and drew the line from *sun* to the picture of a sun. Ashton tried to follow the tape, but Peley would print messy letters and words quickly and go ahead. Ashton would say, "You're going too fast! Wait!" Mrs. Gerard would hear him, come over to the station and say, "Peley, slow down. I know you know the letters, but you must wait for Ashton. You can wait, can't you? I'll test you soon." Peley would stop, frown and wait. Mrs. Gerard would return and test the children on the words they wrote on the page. Peley usually received a perfect score.

Raji would follow the tape in the work journal station and write his letters neatly, but again, he complained about the earphones' loud volume. Also, when the taped voice said, "think" or "thank," "th, th," Raji couldn't figure out the *th* sound. "What is it? What letter? I don't know the sound." When Mrs. Gerard was called over, she vocalized the sound, showing Raji with her mouth. He couldn't seem to say or hear the sound. He would write the letters, but appear puzzled. He also reversed and twisted letters *b* and *d, p, g,* and *j* and *s* and *z,* but his spelling progress was excellent. During one testing session, Mrs. Gerard directed him to make a story with the word *snake.* He wrote:

    snaks hew skin
    snaks Et wrms

Raji did much of his storywriting during tests at the end of a unit in his work journal. Mrs. Gerard praised him, but he never shared the stories with the class.

Make Words Station. The make words station was filled with games that gave practice in word recognition and making new words through rhyming words and grapheme-phoneme connections. Raji was paired with many of his classmates at this station and had difficulties with the games.

Playing the Puppy-word Game with Eric demonstrated Raji's problems with sight words. An oak-tag, laminated brown puppy with a pocket in the back of its head and around its belly contained sight words to be studied. Students would take sight words from its head, and if pronounced properly, the words would be placed in the belly pocket. Eric could name all of the words easily, but Raji, by the middle of the school year, was unable to name the following words: *away, orange, we, school, the, yellow.* He would figure out the beginning sounds and then quietly say, "I don't like this game. I don't want to do this."

At the make words station, children were also encouraged to write on the blackboard. Raji would ask a student at the board, "How do you make *you*? How do you make *you*?" He was heard, observed and ignored. Therefore, he would usually copy what other students wrote on the blackboard. Just as in the computer center, he also made many visits to the bathroom.

At the make words station, Peley would write words on the blackboard copied from the girls next to her. She would listen and watch them talking to each other. If they wrote "mother"or "I love you," Peley watched and wrote the same. Ashton was again paired with her for the make words games. He would become agitated at this station and ask, "What do we do here?" Peley would ignore him and pick up the folder on the table to figure out the day's game.

One day in the spring, Mrs. Gerard was near the table and explained, "Take out the cards and match all *H* words on the hippopotamus and all the *W* words on the walrus." A large laminated hippopotamus card and walrus card with pockets in the front allowed them to place the appropriate word cards in the pockets. The word cards had picture clues on them and were kept in a separate envelope, but these only confused Ashton. He called a watermelon picture card "banana" and a web picture card "spider web." Neither fit the *H* or *W* and he was puzzled. Peley finished her hippopotamus easily and said, "Give me your card. I'm done." Ashton responded with frustration, "Peley, you go too fast. You don't wait for me." Mrs. Starr came over to the table and told the two children to switch the walrus for the hippopotamus. Peley then finished the walrus, focused her eyes on activities in the other centers and made no attempt to help Ashton. Mrs. Gerard saw Peley and called both children to the computer center. Peley slowly moved to the station while Ashton skipped to the spot, positioned his earphones, and began the program.

Reading whole stories was another important part of the writing-to-read program. This took place at the listening library or the book browsing boat stations. Neither contained multicultural literature related to Southeast Asia or India.

Listening Library. The listening library contained earphones, cassettes and books for listening and reading. This was Raji's favorite station. He loved the book, *A Snowy Day*, by Ezra Jack Keats. Raji explained, "The boy looks like me." The book was in the station for only a week, but Raji would follow along, carefully listening to the words on the cassette. He would sometimes mouth the words and point to them on the page. Peley on the other hand would not follow tapes in this station. She flipped through the pages, selected certain words, and pronounced them. She would finish the book before the tape ended and remove the earphones. Then she'd check around for another book or ask to go to another station.

Book Browsing Boat. The book browsing boat was heaped with children's literature for free reading time. If Peley was left alone with Ashton, she would first pretend to row the boat. Then she would quickly flip through pages of several books. If she found a Dr. Seuss book, such as *The Foot Book,* she would read a few pages aloud and ask for help on the words she couldn't sound out or figure out from the pictures. When Peley was asked if she would like to read to someone or be read a book of her own choosing, she would ignore the questions or shake her head in the negative. However, when Ashton was read a story in the boat, Peley would eventually drop her book and concentrate on the story read by the teacher. Other children regularly requested read- alouds from the teacher.

Raji was attentive in the book boat. He would select a book and study each page carefully. He never asked an adult to read with him, but he listened to any story being read. He especially liked the pop-up predictable storybook entitled *The Wheels On The Bus* by Zelinski. People representing different ethnic groups were on the bus riding through a small city. The children including Raji laughed and responded to the repetition.

The main connection between the writing-to-read lab and the kindergarten classroom was during share time. The children in the top group wrote stories at the writing/typing station and at the writing/drawing table. They volunteered to read their stories in the regular classroom right after they returned from lab. The average group, taught in the kindergarten classroom, also shared their stories at that time.

Writing/Typing Station. The writing/typing station consisted of computers with a word processing program. The children joyfully typed, saved, and printed their own stories using invented spelling. The teacher or assistant would converse with a child about a topic before writing began. Often, Peley could not think of a topic, so she would write her first and last name, the date and shut off the computer. The teacher would see what she had done and reboot the computer. Peley would then copy words from the screen next to her.

Finally, in January, she wrote her first original story on the computer. Most of the children in the group had been composing for weeks. At the station, Peley informed the teacher, "I don't like it here." Mrs. Starr responded with, "Let's think of a story." Peley whined. "I don't like this." Mrs. Starr continued, "Why don't you write about what you like? Who do you like?" Peley smiled and her first story was typed on the computer.

Peley Lom 1/16 MY LIKE STORY
I like joe
Evin I like
Mrs. str
I like MY Brathr

This was a new experience for Peley. Her confidence rose when she shared her next story with the class.

Peley 1/24 My NIS STOREY
I AM Siley.
My Brathr is.
Varey Nis.

When classmates laughed and clapped, Peley's interest in story writing on the computer piqued.

2/23
My brotthr seys I am
Clamzey and I Like being
Cold Clomzey.
I say to My Self
Me and My Big Mowf.
And I go Wakey Like go go do do

3/19
ME AND MY BIG MOUTH
AND EVEIN
ANT I A STINGKER.

The class howled; Peley was delighted with their enthusiasm and continued the theme of big mouth and stinker for the rest of the school year.

Raji occasionally wrote stories at the writing, typing computer station. It took him a lot of time and teacher attention to type his stories. The following is a portion of the dialogue between Raji and Mrs. Starr as she guided his writing:

Mrs. Starr: Raji, what are you going to write about?
Raji: I don't know.
Mrs. Starr: Let's see, hmmm, why don't you write about your family. I know you love your mom and dad. You could write about them.

Raji shook his head in agreement; Mrs. Starr left his side. Raji began typing. "I Love mom I love ded"

The next day Mrs. Starr arrived at his side and praised him for his story.

Mrs. Starr: This is a nice story Raji. Why do you love your mom and dad? What do they do for you ?
Raji: They help me.
Mrs. Starr: Yes, because [emphasized], they help you!

Mrs. Starr left Raji again; that day he typed, "becos tha help me"

The following day, Mrs. Starr returned and expressed her pleasure with his work.

Mrs. Starr: Raji, yes! You love your mom and dad because they help you. You almost have a story. Remember, a story has to have three sentences. Who else is in your family? Don't you have a sister?

Raji shook his head positively as the teacher left. He wrote, "Deez is my sitr"

After three sessions at the typing/writing station, Raji completed the story on April 7. He did not ask to share the story with the class. A month later, he typed numbers from 1 to 62. Other students in this class were typically typing a whole story during one session. Both Raji and Peley, if given a choice, preferred other stations.

Writing/Drawing Table. Finally, the writing/drawing table

located in the center of the lab provided opportunities to write and read. Students were given white, blank lined paper shapes, such as a tooth, snowman, fish, or pumpkin. They would write about the shape or anything else in their minds, using invented spelling. They would proudly read their stories to teachers, or each other or bring them back to the classroom for sharing. Peley wrote, talked to her neighbors, and shared her stories, but she was often critical of their work. When the class began to appreciate her stories, her time around the table seemed less of a struggle. The following activities and transcripts show her development.

At the table, in January, Mrs. Gerard gave Peley's group large, tooth-shaped booklets. The tooth-shaped cover of the booklet had eyes, nose, and smiling mouth. The children colored the cover and wrote stories inside on the lined paper about losing teeth or visiting the dentist. Peley's own teeth had obvious,   brown decayed areas, unlike any of the other children's teeth.

The following dialogue was recorded while the children composed in the tooth-shaped booklets:

```
     Peley:    What do you write?
     Nancy:    About teeth.
     Peley:    Why?
     Linda:    It's a tooth!!!
     Peley:    I don't want to write that.
[Peley looks over at Nancy's story.]
     Peley:    Your story is stinky.
[Nancy appears to ignore her.]
     Peley:    Mrs. Starr, do I have to write about the tooth?
Mrs. Starr:   No, Peley.  You may write about anything.
     Peley:    Why do we have this tooth?
[Mrs. Starr didn't seem to hear the question.]
```

Peley composed her story and colored the tooth cover quickly. She wrote the following on January 8:

```
IT is a suney
day.  I LOVE MY MOM
A LOT. varey mack
AND I LOVE MY daD
varey mack
A LOT TO I,LIC
```

My Fred

Peley was asked to share the story, but could not be heard while she read it to the class. The teacher helped her with several words.

In February, Peley was sent to the writing table while Mrs. Gerard cut out a 9" x 14" yellow fish. She drew lines across it and handed it to Peley.

Mrs. Gerard: Peley, write a story about a fish.
      Peley: I don't want to. I don't like fish.
Mrs. Gerard: Tell me what a fish does.
      Peley: [Frown and folded arms.]
Mrs. Gerard: Do you like to eat fish?
      Peley: No! My grandmother eats fish!!

Mrs. Gerard left the scene leaving Peley staring at the fish. Five minutes later Mrs. Gerard returned.

Mrs. Gerard: Peley, you must write three sentences. Now, let's get started.
[Peley, with a frown, angrily began to scribble and then wrote.]

MY PET IS QUT
FISH
R Nis.

Peley finished writing, dropped her pencil on the table, put her head down and complained of a sick stomach.

By the end of the school year, Peley discovered that if she wrote stories in her booklets that included negative comments at her expense, she could get the table to laugh.

Peley: Listen Linda. I can say this Me and My big mouth aint I a stinky.
[The children around the table laugh; some look over at her writing.]
Annie: You are so funny. Say it again!
Matt: Peley, I can't stop laughing.

Peley willingly began sharing her stories in the classroom after writing-to-read lab. She became the class comedienne by making fun of herself or her family:

I can say this Me and My big mouth aint I a stinky and I can say Mom I love you varry much I love you to much that I cood screem varry loud. Mom I love you to much varry much I love you and you look nise Mom I think you are the best mom in the wrld mom you look Byootfl mom and I love you.

When given the choice between typing or writing the stories, Peley preferred writing the stories at the writing table. By June her stories were as lengthy as the other children's. She also made booklets with pictures to accompany her print.

Raji preferred to draw and color at the writing, drawing table. When he returned from India in February, Mrs. Starr questioned him about India and gave him extra help with his story writing. They practiced grapheme-phoneme connections for invented spelling while he sat and typed at the computer station. She cut his story into strips of words and taped them into a booklet shaped like the country of India. Each sentence strip appeared on a page of the booklet where Raji drew pictures with colored magic markers. They worked daily for two weeks on the following story:

India
It is hot in India.
Santimz in India it is cold.
I nevr so sno in India.

A week after writing his story, Raji volunteered to read it during classroom sharing. He could not read many of the words without the teacher's help. Mrs. Starr explained to the class, "India was where Raji was while he was gone for so long. He says there is no snow in India and it is hot. That's great Raji." No comments or questions came from his classmates, so Mrs. Starr directed the children to line up for music class.

Raji did not have many opportunities to work in the writing, drawing center, because his teachers believed he needed help with grapheme-phoneme connections. But, when given the choice between the writing, typing station and the writing, drawing table, he chose the writing, drawing table. His last story of the year featured a booklet cover with a brightly colored frog on a lily pad. It had been drawn and cut out by the teacher, but Raji had chosen greens, purples and pinks to meticulously color it with magic markers and crayons. He wrote on May 27:

I. LiK. frogs. Bicos.
THey.   and.

THey. MaKe.
nose. and They
hav. a. lag ad
THey. Hop. on
LiLY Pads.

Raji enjoyed drawing and coloring the booklets for stories he wrote. When asked what was his favorite thing to do in school, he always replied, "Drawing" or "Coloring" or "Painting" or "Clay." But he rarely shared his work, even though Mrs. Starr tried to encourage him.

Differences between home and school cultures were not addressed in the writing-to-read program. No literature from the children's cultures was included and neither child seemed able to connect with topics around the writing/drawing table. Peley and Raji took longer to begin their stories and longer to finish their stories as they stared at paper or computer screen. Peley's tooth story and Raji's family story were examples of the tedious times they experienced, taking weeks to complete a few lines while staring at the computer or paper. Peley finally joined the community of writers through her self-deprecating stories. She was able to make meaning by stimulating laughter. Raji never joined.

Summary and Evaluation of Literacy Learning

Peley and Raji struggled through the learning centers, literacy activities, reading group, ESL classes, and writing-to-read lab. Mrs. Starr saw their struggles, but since they seemed to be making adequate progress in relation to the rest of the group, she was not alarmed. Both children were reading and writing stories by the end of the school year. Peley was reading self-selected books by January; Raji could read many words in the literature-based series. Mrs. Starr was pleased with the children's literacy learning progress but couldn't figure out why they didn't make friends.

Similar to emergent literacy studies (Wells, 1986; Dyson, 1989), Mrs. Starr attempted to create a community of readers and writers. During learning center activities, reading in pairs, writing lab collaboration, and class share time, she promoted meaning- making among the children. She encouraged class participation when children read to each other, asked questions, presented their writing, and shared home activities. But Peley and Raji did not seem to be members of the classroom community; Mrs. Starr was baffled. When Peley read a book in class, she was alone. When Raji shared his story of India, no connections were made with classmates. He never shared his home activities.

Furthermore, the two children's ESL pull-out program occurred twice a week during reading group. This deficit or subtractive ESL model for English literacy development (Cummins, 1986; Fishman, 1989) promoted cultural conflict and produced struggles for Mrs. Starr and the children. Peley and Raji were the only two children removed from the class for special help. Additionally, the ESL program was not coordinated with the kindergarten program. Peley, in particular, showed her dislike when she left the classroom. Her reactions negatively accentuated her differences.

Mrs. Starr struggled with the idea that the ESL teacher knew what was best for the children and wondered about the children missing valuable reading and special project time. She saw Peley and Raji making progress, but losing continuity. She had no opportunity to meet with the ESL teacher to discuss program, so she did not know what was being taught.

Finally, the writing-to-read lab had both positive and negative influences on the children's literacy learning. Raji worked alone at the computer station and work journal stations, because he had been in India for two months and needed to catch up with the rest of the group. He seemed to have difficulty concentrating at those stations, because he often left for the bathroom or a drink during that time. He also complained that the earphones were too loud. He completed most of the written work at the work journal station, but consistently twisted and reversed several letters. At the make words station, he didn't know many of the words used in the games, so he had little success. He rarely wrote stories on his own at the writing/drawing table or on the computers. However, he drew and colored many pictures at the writing/drawing table. Raji enjoyed the book boat and the listening library, the least popular stations for the other children in the computer lab. He smiled while listening with earphones and followed along in story books.

Peley was impatient while working at the stations. The earphones seemed to slow her thinking. However, she quickly learned grapheme-phoneme connections for consonant sounds and many blends and also began to learn vowel patterns. She was also impatient with partners at many of the stations, because she knew how to easily complete tasks and games. She made every effort to avoid the computers and preferred the writing/drawing table in the center of the lab. By the end of the year, she made the children laugh around the table with the "funny" stories about herself and family.

When Mrs. Gerard and Mrs. Starr evaluated each student according to the progress made at the stations, Peley was considered an excellent story writer and reader. Raji, however, was considered inconsistent in his writing-to-read work. Mrs. Gerard believed Raji should participate in the summer maintenance program for his language learning.

Mrs. Starr believed the students in the top group had made remarkable progress in reading. She wondered about their thoughts concerning reading. When the students were seated around tables in groups of five or six while writing in their kindergarten graduation booklets, they were asked, "Can you tell me about your reading?" The following are replies from a table of students in the top group.

Jimmy:	It's words and sounds.
Annie:	It's books; I read at home.
Peley:	It's reading group, and I read at home.
Raji:	I don't know.
Nanci:	It's writing stories
Jennifer:	It's reading books and reading group.
Jerry:	It's reading group.

When Raji was asked again, he shrugged his shoulders. He didn't seem to know how to talk about reading. Peley differentiated between reading in reading group and reading at home.

At the end of the school year, Peley and Raji were tested by the building reading teacher. Peley was placed in the top first grade reading group. Raji was placed in an average group. Both students were also recommended for continuation in the ESL program since their scores on a language assessment test, given by the ESL teacher, indicated needs.

It was also suggested by the kindergarten staff that Raji attend the summer literacy maintenance program funded by the school district. The kindergarten through second grade students recommended for this program were given integrated literacy experiences related to hands-on work and play activities and field trips. Mrs. Starr believed that Raji should be enrolled lest he lose the skills he had learned in kindergarten. She was worried about his apparent lack of interest during reading group and inability to understand what was happening.

Mrs. Starr did not worry about Peley's reading because she thought that Peley had experienced success. However, she worried about Peley's social development and hoped she would have opportunities to interact with children from East Side Elementary School during a neighborhood summer day camp program.

Mrs. Starr did not seem to realize that Peley's and Raji's struggles might be due to cultural conflict and the inability to connect home and school cultures. She took note of some obvious visible signs of struggle during holidays and classroom celebrations, but she thought they would eventually learn to fit in by observing the other children in the classroom community. The following chapter describes the children's cultural conflicts and struggles during classroom celebrations.

Confused by Halloween, Peley colored her face red, wore a molded plastic, blonde, princess mask and called herself "Barbie Doll."

5

Tinsel and Tension: Holidays and Celebrations

Like many early childhood programs across the United States, East Side Elementary School celebrated Columbus Day, Halloween, Thanksgiving, Christmas, New Year's, Valentine's Day, Presidents' birthdays, St. Patrick's Day, and Easter. Additionally, because the school community had customs primarily related to the Roman Catholic tradition, secular and religious aspects of school celebrations often became blurred. Furthermore, the seasons of the year were interwoven into the holidays. Colored construction paper cut-outs taped to the windows of the school signaled special times several weeks before the date; hallways and classrooms were decorated with representative symbols.

September windows displayed autumn leaves, apples and pumpkins, October classrooms exhibited Columbus artwork and Halloween ghosts and goblins, November halls showed pilgrims, turkeys and Native Americans, and December saturated the senses with silver and gold tinsel and red and green colors. January emphasized winter, with snow flakes, sleds, and polar bears positioned throughout the school. As February approached, the polar bears carried red valentines; these were replaced with shamrocks for St. Patrick's Day. Easter rabbits appeared immediately after March 17, and finally, large cut-out daisies, tulips, and daffodils announced spring and early summer.

The kindergarten classrooms were decorated with tinsel, crepe paper, and shiny foil letters announcing each holiday. The curriculum revolved around literature, music, games, and arts and crafts related to the upcoming special time; classroom parties were arranged and parents contributed refreshments and helping hands during the celebrations. Along with the holidays, kindergarten classrooms celebrated birthdays, marvelous Mother's Day, fabulous Father's Day, pajama day and kindergarten Olympics. This plethora of special days served to keep the classroom in perpetual anticipation of the next festivity.

Home and school were connected in the classroom as mothers helped in the preparations and festivities. However, these celebrations often caused confusion for Peley, Raji, and their families. They sincerely attempted to understand the customs of the dominant culture represented in the school, but many practices in their homes differed from the school including the holidays and celebrations. The resulting cultural conflict between home practices and school expecations produced struggles. Research suggests (Ogbu, 1987; Skutnabb-Kangas & Cummins, 1988; Fishman, 1989; Trueba, 1989) that when the home culture is ignored or neglected, language-minority students become bewildered. Similarly,when misunderstandings of holidays and celebrations were obvious, Peley and Raji became visible. They did not fit into the classroom culture and were considered problems. Mrs. Starr noticed the children's struggles in the fall and believed they would eventually learn to fit in by participating in the year's special events. This chapter presents examples of the children's struggles to understand the holidays and celebrations in the kindergarten program.

Columbus Day

Columbus Day echoed the traditional story, songs, and activities practiced in the schools of the United States during most of the last century. Stories were read aloud in class and the music teacher taught Columbus songs. Each child made construction paper cut-and-paste Columbus-ships-in-a-bottle to take home.

The ESL teacher, Mrs. Brown tried to explain the Columbus discovery story to Peley and Raji. She laid a map of the World on the round table in the ESL classroom and began pointing out India and Cambodia. Peley immediately sprawled over it, while Raji sat in a chair.

Mrs. Brown:	Peley, this is Cambodia. This is where your family lived. Isn't that right? Were you born in Cambodia?
Peley:	[Indignantly] No! I was born in the United States. I was born in the United States! My mother told me!
Mrs. Brown:	[Calmly] Fine Peley. Raji, were you born in India?
Raji:	[Softly] I don't know.
Mrs. Brown:	[While pointing at the World map] Now here is Cambodia.
Peley:	[Immediately interjects loudly] I was born in the United States! I was born in the United States.
Mrs. Brown:	[Calmly] I know, Peley, and here's India.

[Mrs. Brown moved her finger from India to Spain.]

Mrs.Brown: [Enthusiastically] Columbus sailed from Spain and discovered America!

[Mrs. Brown moved her finger across the Atlantic Ocean to the United

States.]

Mrs. Brown: He came to America just like your family. That's why we celebrate Columbus Day.

[Neither Raji nor Peley responded to the statement. Mrs. Brown then brought out a globe, night light.]

Mrs. Brown: This is my son's night light, but he let me bring it to school. You can see the World is round. Raji, put your finger on India and we'll turn the globe to find America, where we live.

[Raji put his finger on India and then he put the finger from his other hand on America.]

Peley: [Pleading] Let me try! Let me try!

[Mrs. Brown helped her put fingers on Cambodia and America.]

Peley: [Immediately after] I want to play the vowel game. I want to play the vowel game! Pleeease!

Mrs. Brown: [Emphatically] No, Peley, not until Thursday. There isn't enough time.

Peley: [Pleading] I want to write on the board. I want to write on the board!

Mrs. Brown: [Exasperated tone] Okay, but you must practice writing your names.

[Raji wrote on the blackboard "Raji" making the "R" extra large. Peley quickly wrote "Peley Lom Chinh".]

Mrs. Brown: Chinh? Peley, is that your name too. I thought your name was Peley Lom?

Peley: [Emphatically and loudly] No! My name is Peley Lom Chinh! Peley Lom Chinh! That's my real name!

Mrs. Brown: [Calmly] All right, Peley and Raji, time to go back to class.

Both children immediately dropped their pieces of chalk and raced to the door. Mrs. Brown warned them to wait for her and reminded them about not running in the halls. The children ignored her.

Mrs. Brown believed the children did not understand her Columbus lesson. She was also annoyed with Peley's behaviors. "She takes over the class and Raji doesn't say anything. She is a difficult child. I wonder where she was born. Do her parent's speak any English? What's her real name?" Mrs. Brown also seemed to realize that she knew very little about Peley's and Raji's backgrounds.

Halloween

Immediately after Columbus Day, ghosts, witches, jack-o'-lanterns, and skeletons materialized throughout East Side Elementary School. As October 31 approached more drawings, cutouts, and pieces of children's literature became visible from the second floor library to the basement music room. Songs, books, videos, and math games reflected the coming event. Notes went home for refreshments and party plans. Discussions about costumes and scary creatures occupied sharing time, the discovery center spider unit and teacher read-aloud time.

"What are ya gonna be Halloween?" Annie asked as five children were making their pipe cleaner spiders at the discovery center. "I'm a princess." "I'm gonna be a witch." "Little Mermaid." "I'm a football player."

While making the paper ghosts, another group talked about their costumes. "I'm a queen." "I'm a Ninja turtle, Michelangelo." "My mom bought me a bat costume." "I'm a little devil." "Will you wear a mask?" "Nope! My mom's painting my face. It's safer." "I'm wearing a turtle mask. It fits my face good." The teaching assistant asked Peley, "What are you going to be?" Peley didn't answer.

The interpretations of Halloween seemed to demonstrate cultural confusion and struggle for Peley. On Halloween day, Peley arrived in school with her face painted red; she carried a tube of red lipstick. Her costume was a rumpled, tattered commercial Halloween costume of white rayon satin. It fit so tightly over her jeans and T-shirt, the seams barely held together. Her molded plastic mask was a blonde, blue-eyed princess complete with a yellow, plastic crown. Peley immediately went to a mirror in the bathroom and put more lipstick on her lips. She then placed the mask over her face and announced that she was "Barbie Doll." Classmates repeatedly asked, "Who are you?" Peley would remove her mask exposing her red painted face and pronounce emphatically, "Barbie Doll."

Most students wore newly purchased costumes and masks which they removed from bright boxes. A few home-crafted costumes suggested hours of parental preparation. Disguises included a dog, bear, bat, gypsy, bride, queen, fairy godmother, devil, cat, pumpkin, and several ghosts, witches, pirates, and Ninja Turtles. One student's face was an artistically painted green Ninja Turtle. Raji also appeared as a Ninja Turtle. He wore his red pajamas and carried a green molded plastic turtle mask. When asked which turtle he represented he quietly responded, "Raphael."

Mrs. Starr began the Halloween celebration when several mothers with refreshments came through the door. The mothers immediately went to their own children and gave them hugs and costume adjustments. Mrs. Starr then gathered the masqueraded assembly around the big brown rug. Each student was asked to come forward and explain his or her disguise. Mrs. Starr made a positive comment about each.

Raji's costume was appropriate for the Halloween party, but Peley seemed confused about the concept of wearing a mask and painting one's face. She knew "Barbie" as an important children's doll, but didn't know how to portray "Barbie" in costume. Halloween was difficult for her.

Thanksgiving

Turkeys, Native American head bands, and Pilgrim hats materialized by the end of the first week in November. Thanksgiving preparations began with stories about the first Thanksgiving, and the production of Pilgrim hats and feathered headdresses. Songs about turkeys and feasts were rehearsed. After one story about Thanksgiving, the teacher and children discussed the meaning of the word "thankful." Next, the class was given an assignment to draw a picture about the Thanksgiving story or things we are thankful for at Thanksgiving. The children drew pictures of Native Americans, Pilgrims, turkeys, families, money, birthday parties and so on.

Raji's crayon drawing depicted a table with fish on it. Fish were never mentioned in the story or discussion. Students near him commented, "Fish for Thanksgiving! Yucky!", "Nobody eats fish for Thanksgiving!" Raji's family, as vegetarians, ate seafood, a diet typical of people from Bombay, India. Peley drew a picture of herself as the elegant Asian woman in a long dress and called it "sister." Peley had an older brother, but no sister. The meaning of Thanksgiving in the United States seemed a puzzle to both children.

Raji left the United States soon after Thanksgiving to visit relatives in India for two months. Peley's problems with holidays and special days continued.

Christmas

By the first week in December, Christmas in the school and kindergarten classrooms was glitter and tinsel, red Santas and green trees, reindeer and candy canes, wreathes and holly, bows and wrapped gifts. Additionally, the parent organization of the school also sponsored the Christmas Store as a money-making project. It provided Christmas shopping opportunities for the children with new and used small items costing less than a dollar.

Mrs. Starr reported that Peley's father had come to the Christmas Shop and purchased gifts with Peley.

Because of numerous extra activities added to the kindergarten day during the week before Christmas, presents were made for parents during reading group time. A memorable scene from one session demonstrates Peley's frustrations.

First, Mrs. Starr read a poem about two hands helping, typed on a sheet of white paper; there was no discussion of the poem. She then began, "When I call your name we are going to make Christmas presents for your parents. While you are waiting, you may read and share books quietly with a friend."

Mrs. Starr had placed big books of *Old MacDonald* and *Mother Goose* and little book copies on the rug where the reading group usually met. The children immediately paired or tripled. Peley took the *Old MacDonald* big book to the edge of the rug and hid behind it while reading the words to herself. She remained there as children were called individually or volunteered. Each child was allowed to choose a piece of red, green or blue construction paper. Then the child's hands were placed in white paste, palms down and imprinted on the construction paper. The poem was then glued between the hands.

All of the students had their hands imprinted and class time was nearing the end when Mrs. Starr noticed Peley behind the big book and exclaimed, "I didn't get your hands, Peley!" Peley slowly stood up and walked to the table. She frowned and said, "Yuk!" Mrs. Starr responded, "Peley, don't you want a Christmas present for your parents?" Peley did not reply. Mrs. Starr placed Peley's brown hands in the white paste. Peley continued making her "Yuk" sounds and quickly washed her hands after the imprint. The bell rang as Peley's white hands dried on the blue paper.

Peley's struggle seemed apparent when she hid behind the big book. She was not happy about placing her hands in the paste; a Christmas gift for her parents was meaningless. During a visit to Peley's home a few days before Christmas, there appeared to be no visible signs of the holiday inside or outside her house.

New Year's Day

The second day back to school after Christmas vacation, Peley faced another holiday. In her ESL class, Mrs. Brown attempted to explain New Year's celebrations. She showed Peley a picture of a New Year's Party. The people in the picture had party hats and horns. Food, drinks, and decorations abounded. People were dancing singing and looking happy. Mrs. Brown began the lesson.

Mrs. Brown: Peley, have you ever been to a New Year's Party?
[Peley looked at the picture.]
        Peley: Which hat is different? [pause] Which hat is wrong?
Mrs. Brown: See the horns. Find the one you like.
[Peley did not respond]
Mrs. Brown: Would you like me to read you a story about the picture?"
        Peley: [Loudly] No, I'm hungry!
Mrs. Brown: Didn't you have breakfast?
[Peley shook her head in the negative]
Mrs. Brown: If you want to do well in school, you must eat breakfast.

Mrs. Brown began reading a story to Peley about the history of New Year's Eve. Peley paid no attention. She left her seat and walked to the book shelf. Mrs. Brown called her back and continued the story. Next, Peley blurted, "I want to play a game!" Mrs. Brown, with an impatient tone in her voice, asked, "Peley, do you want to leave?" Peley's enthusiastic response was, "Yes!"

Peley seemed unable to relate to New Year's Eve as it was presented. The teacher/student struggle for understanding seemed apparent in this brief exchange.

Valentine's Day
The next major holiday arrived in mid-January. Hearts of every size and shade of red decorated the school. Silver and gold tinsel, foil-trimmed hearts, and pink and red paper chains filled the kindergarten. On Valentine's Day, the children wore red and white shirts, skirts, dresses, or heart pins. Peley wore her jeans and a blue turtle neck, but the party proved successful for her. She wrote Valentines to the whole class and was able to deliver them personally to her classmates or their mailbags. She was one of the few kindergarteners capable of reading and writing at such an advanced level. Many of the students thanked her for the Valentines as she personally delivered them. She was doubly pleased to see that she had received so many cards in her mailbag. The Valentine's Party appeared to be a victory. Mrs. Starr was pleased to see Peley fitting in and expressed joyfully, "Isn't Peley having a wonderful time?! It's great to see her so happy with herself!"

Mrs. Starr was unaware that red is the color of love and friendship in many Asian cultures. Peley and her family could see the connection between their customs and Valentine's Day.

Marvelous Mother's Day

Raji had returned to the United States from India the week before Valentine's Day, but re-entry into the kindergarten class did not occur until the week following Valentine's Day. On Monday morning, his arrival was greeted with preparations for Marvelous Mother's Day. *M* was the letter for the third week in February, which was to culminate in a Friday celebration especially for mothers.

Discussion of Marvelous Mother's Day produced tears and anxious reactions from several children. Teary-eyed boys and girls openly expressed their concerns to Mrs. Starr. "I don't have a mother." "My mother has to work." "My mother can't leave my baby sister." "My mother can't come." Mrs. Starr responded with, "Bring a marvelous friend or ask your father or grandmother to come. One child stated, "I don't have a marvelous friend and my mother and father can't come." Mrs. Starr tried to soothe their concerns, "I'll be your friend! You can bring anyone you want."

Marvelous Mother's Day had a specific scheme. Children were told to think about their marvelous mothers or friends and tell marvelous things about them. On the day before the celebration, children made crayon drawings of their "marvelous mothers" or friends with the marvelous things they do pictured around them. At the party, the children were told that they would tell about their marvelous mothers or friends. Then their guests would find the pictures of themselves created by the children and stapled to a Marvelous bulletin board.

While Peley and Raji were at ESL class, the kindergarten children received instructions for Marvelous Mother's Day. When Peley and Raji returned to class, they were told to quickly draw a picture of their mothers for Marvelous Mother's Day. Peley responded, "My mother and father can't come." Mrs. Starr then asked, "How about your grandmother?" Peley didn't respond, but began the picture. When asked about her drawing, she said, "It's my grandmother."

On Marvelous Mother's Day, fathers, mothers, grandparents, and friends were seated in a circle on the big brown rug. Miss Corky, the teen kindergarten aide, was assigned as Peley's marvelous friend. Mrs. Starr also became Jeffy's marvelous friend, since he claimed to have no marvelous friend to bring to school. Mrs. Starr positioned herself in front of the squirming mass of adults seated in kindergarten chairs with children at their feet and in their laps. Some children were also standing between adult knees. Peley sat on the floor in front of Miss Corky's chair. Next to Peley, Raji sat alone in front of an empty chair, waiting for his mother. Mrs. Starr began the party five minutes later in the hope that Raji's mother would arrive soon. She asked Raji, "Raji, are you sure your mother is coming?" Raji nodded in the affirmative. Soon after the exchange, Raji's mother and three-year-old sister tiptoed into the classroom. Mrs. Fuller, the teaching assistant, ushered her to the chair in the circle. At that point, the children were about half way around the circle describing marvelous mothers and friends.

When it was Peley's turn to tell about her marvelous friend, Miss Corky, she didn't speak. Her picture had been about her grandmother. Mrs. Starr quickly moved on to Raji. His mother and sister sat in the chair behind him. Mrs. Starr asked, "Raji, do you want to talk about your marvelous mother? She's right behind you. Think about your picture." Raji remained silent and Mrs. Starr moved on with, "Okay, thank you Raji." Raji and Peley were the only two children who did not speak.

When refreshments were served, Raji, his mother, and sister sat together in the corner of the room while other children and adults mingled. Peley sat alone. Her marvelous teen friend was talking with another teen across the room. This celebration seemed to be yet another struggle for both Raji and Peley.

St. Patrick's Day

Preparation for St. Patrick's Day began two weeks before the party. Mrs. Starr delighted the class with her imaginary "Lucky the Leprachaun." Lucky invaded the classroom each morning before the children arrived and accomplished mischievous acts. On the first morning, Lucky Leprachaun walked through green paint and left foot prints throughout the room. The following days, he dumped waste baskets, messed up book shelves and scribbled on the blackboards with green chalk. The children were challenged to figure out how to make him behave. Irish tales were read and songs were sung, with green dominating the classroom world.

On St. Patrick's Day, two children in the class did not wear green, Raji and Tim. Tim had been absent for the last week. Comments were made by the children, "No green!" "Where's the green?" "You're not St. Patrick's." Raji did not respond. He apparently did not get the message about the importance of wearing green on St. Patrick's Day. Peley, however, wore a green turtle neck sweater.

Easter

The day after the St. Patrick's celebration, floppy-eared, beribboned Easter rabbits materialized everywhere in the school. A bulletin board saying "Spring has hatched"appeared at the entrance of Mrs. Starr's room. Even though Easter was a month away, the wire across the room was hung with pink, foil letters announcing, "Happy Easter." Many projects were developed around Easter and the signs of spring. The children saw eggs hatch in an incubator. They cut and pasted paper eggs, flowers, birds, and rabbits.

In a discussion about the picture book, *Signs of Spring*, the children responded to the question "What is a sign of spring?" Peley answered, "Snow melting." Raji answered, "Trees turn brown." Mrs. Starr corrected, "You mean green, Raji." Other answers from the children were, "eggs," "birds," "flower, and sun."

During that month, the class colored bunnies for a newspaper contest. They learned to write the word *Easter* in the writing-to-read lab and composed numerous stories about Easter, such as, "I like the Easter bunny. He brigs gele bens." "The Easter bunny has eggs." "The Easter bunny hops to my house." Peley and Raji colored bunnies and copied "Easter," but they never wrote or talked about Easter baskets or related traditions. Peley drew a green and red rabbit and wrote, "The rabit is sile It is fall." Raji drew an orange rabbit and wrote, "Rabits hop. et to mch eggs." Easter was yet another holiday that the two children did not seem to understand.

Pajama Party

The pajama party was the culminating activity for the letter "P" week. All teachers, assistants, and children wore their pajamas, nightgowns, robes and slippers to school. Even the principal joined activities for the day wearing her flannel night shirt. Peley wore an adult woman's striped, knit, long-sleeved shirt over her jeans and turtle neck sweater. She wore sneakers on her feet. Raji wore the Ninja Turtle pajamas used as a costume for Halloween and his velcro sneakers. Peley and one other girl, who had been absent for a week, were the only children not wearing pajamas or nightgown. Mrs. Starr wondered about Peley's parent's interpretation of this celebration. She asked, "I wonder what they think we're doing in school? Maybe they think Peley has not understood the assignment."

Birthdays

Birthdays were yet another reason for celebration in this kindergarten classroom. There was a separate birthday cupcake bulletin board with each child's name and date on a construction paper cupcake. When a birthday neared, the teacher communicated with the parents and child to make birthday plans. Discussions took place concerning what refreshments would be served, who would serve, and when they would be served. Mrs. Starr also added that the birthday child could bring a favorite pillow for the birthday spanking. This was the classroom custom of tapping out the child's age, plus one for good luck, on his or her behind. The pillow was supposed to be protection. Mrs. Starr would ask the child to lean over with the pillow held behind. She would clap her hands the correct number while the class counted along. The children would laugh and enjoy the trick.

Raji's birthday was in November. His mother and baby sister brought in cupcakes from a local bakery. They served them with the teacher's help. They watched Raji as the children sang and he was coronated with a personalized birthday crown created by Mrs. Starr. He smiled and maintained his usual calm and quiet composure.

Peley's birthday, however, did not go as smoothly. Her birthday was an event she had been thinking about for at least a month before the date. She repeatedly reminded Mrs. Starr of the date; Mrs. Starr reminded Peley to bring the pillow for the birthday spanking. Peley would also mention that cookies would be the class party treat.

The week before Peley's birthday, several notes were exchanged. Mrs. Starr initiated the process by sending a note home with Peley. The note explained that since her birthday fell on a Saturday, the best time to celebrate would be on the Monday after. This would allow more time for a party. Peley's family sent a note in response; it read as follows:

    Dear Mrs. Starr
    Peley want to share her
    birthday party with her class mate
    On Friday I will send cookies for
    all the children if o.k. for you.
    On 4.3.
    Thank You
    Mrs. Lom

The script was half printed, half cursive and was on the back of a sheet of notebook paper. When Mrs. Starr received the note from Peley, she asked, "Peley, when will you be having the party?" Peley responded, "Friday." Mrs. Starr continued, "But Peley, I wrote your mother a note and told her that Monday would be better. On Friday there won't be enough time. When did you say she was bringing the cookies?" Peley answered in a quiet whisper, "Friday." Mrs. Starr then repeated in an exasperated tone, "Well, Peley, you must realize it will be a short party."

On Friday, Peley complained of a stomach ache during learning center. She was ignored, because it was assumed that birthday excitement was the cause. When the circle of children formed, anticipating the snack in celebration of "the birthday girl's happy day," Peley stood in the middle of the rug next to Mrs. Starr. She wore the birthday crown especially cut out and designed for her by Mrs. Starr. It was made of purple construction paper and each point had a green star. Six stars symbolized six years of age; green and purple were Peley's favorite colors. Peley never brought in her birthday pillow, but Mrs. Starr faked the spanking by clapping hands behind. The class sang "Happy Birthday." Peley never smiled. The birthday snacks never came. The children hurriedly ate graham crackers from the class daily supply as they lined up for music.

The following Tuesday, much to Mrs. Starr's surprise, Peley's father appeared before snack time with a box of vanilla cookies purchased from a store. Mrs. Starr thanked him and allowed Peley to distribute the cookies at snack time. There was no mention of Peley's birthday.

Kindergarten Graduation

The June kindergarten graduation program preparations began in May. In music class, songs were rehearsed. Students were chosen to memorize parts to be recited on stage in the auditeria. Invitations and thank yous were composed and large sheet cakes ordered. Students completed personal yearbooks by drawing pictures of themselves in kindergarten and writing about their favorite things. They also helped the teacher make mortar boards from construction paper in the blue and white school colors.

On graduation morning, the parents, grandparents, brothers and sisters flocked in and packed the auditeria. Most of the students wore new clothes, including Peley, who wore a yellow and black linenlike tailored dress. It needed ironing, but she was proud to tell the girls, "I got a new dress for this." Raji wore his usual outfit, the striped wool sweater and dark cotton trousers, a size too small.

With construction paper mortar boards atop their heads, the students filed into the packed auditeria to the accompaniment of Mr. Percy's piano playing "Pomp and Circumstance." Parents with cameras and camcorders lined the walls. Raji's family was present with camera. Peley's father, equipped with camcorder, recorded the entire ceremony.

The students lined up on stage with the help of teachers, aides, and assistant. They sang the rehearsed songs and said their verses in loud, clear voices. Peley had been selected by Mrs. Starr to recite one of six parts. She had practiced with her classmates for the last two weeks, but was barely heard reciting, "I've learned my words and sounds and had my ups and downs." At the end of the ceremony, the principal spoke and gave awards. Then she handed diplomas to each child marching across the stage.

At the classroom reception, Peley's grandmother attempted to give Peley a brown bag containing a box of graham crackers for the classroom reception. Peley pushed the bag aside and sternly spoke in Cambodian. Grandmother closed the bag quickly and looked down at the floor. Peley's father explained, "She see food on letter. She bring food." Peley's grandmother had misinterpreted the graduation invitation.

The reception was lively. Families mingled with each other and said their thank yous to Mrs. Starr. Raji's family separated and stayed in one part of the room while Peley's grandmother and father stood alone in another part of the room. Mrs. Starr made a point of going to the families and telling them how much she had enjoyed working with their children. Raji's family thanked her and added, "You will see our daughter soon. She will be in kindergarten in two years." Peley's father and grandmother bowed their heads and clearly spoke, "Thank you."

Mrs. Starr was pleased that Peley's and Raji's families had come to graduation. She believed that both children had made great gains in one year and was happy to see the parents recognizing their children's year. However, Mrs. Starr was concerned about the children's continuous socialization problems and confusions about class activities. The visible misunderstandings which occurred during holidays and celebrations seemed to confirm her notions that the children could have problems with their literacy learning next year. But she did

not associate their difficulties with the cultural differences
between home and school.

Summary of Tensions

Mrs. Starr was unaware of Peley's and Raji's home cultures
and the need to make connections. Consequently, Peley and Raji
misunderstood many classroom holidays and celebrations. Their
responses were consistent with the literature on diverse
populations and community building (Barrera, 1992; Au, 1993).
When Peley and Raji seemed to understand the meanings of
certain classroom holidays and celebrations, their struggles were
not visible, but their individual responses varied according to the
festivities.

Confused by Halloween, Peley colored her face red, wore a
molded plastic, blonde, princess mask, and called herself "Barbie
Doll." She was often asked her identity during the class party.
On the other hand, Raji came as a Ninja Turtle, a popular costume
for the boys. After the Thanksgiving story, classmates drew
turkeys, Pilgrims and Native Americans. Peley drew herself; Raji
drew fish on his family table. When making Christmas gifts,
classmates enthusiastically imprinted hands in white paste for
their parents, while Peley hid behind a "big book." Raji's birthday
was celebrated in the customary classroom manner. His mother
brought in treats for the class. Due to misunderstandings related
to language, Peley's treats did not arrive from home for her
birthday. Valentine's Day was a successful experience for Peley,
because she wrote and delivered cards to all of her classmates.
She also received cards. Raji was absent for Valentine's Day and
was one of two children not wearing green on St. Patrick's Day.
For Easter, Peley colored a rabbit green and red and wrote, "sile
rabit." Raji wrote, "Rabits hop" under his orange rabbit. Finally
both children were the only ones who did not speak at the
Marvelous Mother's Day celebration.

When Peley and Raji seemed to understand the meanings of
certain classroom holidays and celebrations, they seemed to fit in.
Their struggles were not visible. However, when they did not
understand, social interactions became a struggle.

Holidays and classroom celebrations are time-consuming
portions of an elementary school curricula. Misunderstanding the
dominant culture's festivities excludes students from large
portions of the school community's activities and values. Mrs.
Starr unknowingly adopted the assimilationist perspective and

assumed that the children would automatically learn to understand the classroom culture's holidays and celebrations simply through participation. She also subtracted or ignored their home cultures (Cummins, 1986). Similarly, Mrs. Brown, the ESL teacher was unaware of the need to connect home and school cultures for classroom understanding.

Therefore, when the children's struggles were noted, their parents were not informed. Unfortunately, there was little home and school communication throughout the school year.

Chapter V deals with the weak home and school communication which allowed cultural conflict to exist and left the children's struggles unattended.

Peley and her family always greeted me at the front door with quick bows and broad smiles.

6

Confusion: Home and School Communication

Home and school connections were primary considerations of the kindergarten staff at East Side Elementary School. Similar to the literature on emerging literacy (Taylor & Dorsey-Gaines, 1988; Sulzby & Teale, 1991; Edwards, 1996), the teachers saw the need to connect home and school for literacy learning. However, they believed that most parents were unaware of the importance of home literacy experiences. The staff consistently commented, "Our children need so much. They don't have the language experiences at home that children in other parts of our school district possess." As the staff developed the kindergarten program, they determined that home and school communication should be a primary goal. Therefore, they made themselves available for scheduled and unscheduled conferences at school and on the phone. Notes from home were immediately answered and parents were enthusiastically invited to observe, visit, participate, and contribute in any way possible in the school or classroom. As a result, parents regularly appeared and were accepted without reservation. The staff also planned special events which promoted parent involvement and created, Kid Sheets, home literacy activities for parent and child interaction and classroom sharing. As a result, home and school communication seemed strong with the exception of Peley's and Raji's families. The staff had difficulties communicating with them; the children's families struggled in their attempts to communicate with the school.

Visiting the children's homes and families produced information about the cultural conflicts and struggles related to home and school communication.

Family Struggles

Peley's family. Peley and her family always greeted me at the front door with quick bows and broad smiles. Mother and Grandmother had short sturdy bodies, and deep, dark brown skin, hair and eyes that proclaimed their strong rural Cambodian background. Her father's skin and hair tones were similar, but he was very thin with a delicate Vietnamese framework. The family's appearance contrasted with the tall, blond, pale, blue-eyed people on their street. Peley's family had lived in the neighborhood for several years, but had not met their neighbors. Peley and her brother did not play with the children on the block; they regularly had problems on the school bus. Peley's mother mentioned that the children on the bus had mocked Peley about her "flat nose." Since then, she had removed her school portrait from the living room wall. Peley and her brother usually preferred television and cartoon videos rather than venturing outside.

A Cambodian dialect was the most common language spoken in the home. Peley had the best command of the English language in her family, so she helped her mother shop for household necessities at a local large food store. They visited a Chinese grocery store to obtain special ingredients for the preferred recipes of their culture. Also, Peley was expected to help her mother and grandmother with all household chores. Peley's brother and father did not have specific tasks, but her father had the major responsibility for home and school communication. These were difficult times for him since he had few opportunities to practice his English.

Raji's family. Raji's family emigrated to the United States from India and resided in an apartment complex which housed several other families from diverse cultural backgrounds. Their black hair and deep brown skin and eyes were not unusual for the area, but they mentioned that Raji had experienced discrimination from the White children at the area playground. He was told, "White boys go first on the slide." When a group of children found a tree frog, Raji was warned, "Black boys can't touch the frog." His parents were concerned about these incidents but hoped Raji would eventually work his way into a group of children so the discrimination would stop.

The family's English was clearly expressed and grammatically correct. They also spoke two Indian dialects in their home. The parents believed their children should know how to speak to their relatives in India for their biannual visits. Additionally, they celebrated the holidays unique to their religion and family customs with other Indian families in the area.

Family Communication Struggles
Family communication with the school was a struggle.

Questions about the ESL program and the children's social interactions occurred, but the parents did not take their concerns to school. When the parents did attempt to communicate with the school, the communication was confused or misunderstood.

ESL program. If the child's second language was English, he or she automatically qualified for special services as a potential learning problem at East Side Elementary. The child was analyzed through kindergarten screening, kindergarten teachers' judgments of classroom performance, the reading teacher's and the ESL teacher's diagnoses. Parental consent determined how much extra help a child could receive. Peley's and Raji's parents wanted them in the ESL classes, but Peley had told her mother she did not like being there. When visiting Peley's home, her mother questioned why Peley disliked going to ESL class.

> Peley not like ESL. Why? She need it. She speak good English. She not understand school way. We not speak English. My English not good. We work day. We work night. Peley need help. Our way different. Peley need ESL for school.

Peley's parents worked day and night shifts and did not have the time to communicate with the school. Also they were unsure of their English and the ways of the school. Peley's mother wanted Peley to succeed and thought the ESL class would help Peley understand school. She saw the ESL class as a way to learn how to fit in.

Raji's parents also wanted him in the ESL classes until they learned that Raji had been missing reading class to attend ESL. They discovered this fact toward the end of the school year and were angry. Raji's father explained,

> Raji speaks English. Sometimes he does not say a word the right way, because of the way we say it, but he should not be away from reading class! He should be in ESL after school. What does the ESL teacher do in the class? I think Raji would not be in the summer school if he had not left reading class.

Raji's mother added, "I wish we knew about ESL class. We don't want him to leave reading!" They were frustrated with the lack of information, but they did not know to whom they should address their concerns. They did not understand the ESL program and they couldn't understand why Raji would be taken out of the classroom to study his English.

Social interactions. Both families had questions about Peley's and Raji's social interactions. Neither family asked the school about their children's struggles. Peley's mother knew Peley wanted a friend. "Peley want friend. Friend in school?" But Peley's mother did not know how to help. By the end of the school year, she was discouraged.

> I do not know friend. I do not know parent. We have custom. They have custom different. Afraid different custom. I not know. Peley do not understand. I not know people. Not good. Peley have cousin. She see cousin, weekend.

Peley's mother feared that Peley would not understand the different cultures. She was unable to help Peley connect home and school with friendships; she was unable to communicate about her daughter's lack of friends in school.

Raji's parents also knew that Raji did not have friends in school, but they noticed a change in his personality while in India. There, he had groups of cousins and friends to play with on a daily basis. After two months, when he returned to his classroom in the United States, he displayed confident behaviors for a few weeks. However, his parents noticed that he soon returned to his shy reserved self. They did not contact the school to question his change in behavior. Raji's father explained,

> Raji played with cousins every day in India. Raji was part of their play. If he could find a group of friends here, he would not have trouble. In a group, he would be safe and have friends. If he is in a group, they will not treat him different.

Raji's parents did not know how to help him connect with the school and make friends.

School Communication Struggles

Mrs. Starr encouraged parent involvement in school activities to strengthen the lines of communication between home and school. However, Raji's and Peley's families struggled with open house, parent conferences, kid sheets, and special events meant to connect the home and school.

Open house. The first fall meeting with parents took place on an evening in September of the school year. Both sets of parents came, but Mrs. Starr reported that communication was a struggle.

> Raji's parents came to the open house; his mother said nothing and the father was very specific. He told me exactly what he wanted for his son. He wanted work every night. He wanted his son to always be attentive and that as his teacher, I must call if there is any problem of any kind, no matter how small. He seemed to demand these requests.

Raji's parents attempted to communicate with Mrs. Starr, but she remarked, "I don't think they understand kindergarten. They're putting too much pressure on their son."

Peley's family also experienced communication problems at the open house. Mrs. Starr reported,

> Peley's family speaks almost no English. When they came to the open house, I know they didn't understand anything. I have a feeling they direct Peley completely. I think they tell her what to say in school, how to act with the teacher and what you must do to please the teacher. I think Peley fakes so much.

Peley's family members were unable to communicate, so Mrs. Starr relied on her own interpretations. Both families left her guessing about them and their children.

Parent conferences. The goal of scheduled parent conferences in school was to develop communication for stronger home and school connections, but these also proved to be times of struggle for the two families. For example, Raji's parents arrived fifteen minutes late for their 1:00 p.m. fall appointment. Mrs. Starr explained to them that the conference would end at 1:30 p.m. since other parents were scheduled immediately after. Mr. Jon responded, "Fine, I could not leave my job when I wished, so that is why we are late." A transcript of a portion of the conference is evidence of the parents' struggle to communicate.

Mrs. Starr:	Raji doesn't talk in class. He'll answer questions when I call on him, but he would rather sit back and listen. He also doesn't talk to the other students.
Mr. Jon:	He doesn't talk about school at home. He won't talk about it.
Mrs. Starr:	Hmmm... That's interesting. Well, let's look at his test results. He knows his body parts except for the elbow, ankle, waist and heel, but you can work on those with him.

His coloring is beautiful! He stays in the lines and cuts on the lines. He knows his shapes, but he calls the oval, oal. He leaves out the v.

Mr. Jon: We don't pronounce the v in our language, so he thinks it's the same in English.

Mrs. Starr: I see! Well, Raji, is in the top reading group! He knows the lower and upper case letters and he has begun to sound out words.

Mrs. Jon: We practice the words at home. Sometimes he says *cat* for *can*, but he is learning.

Mrs. Starr: It shows that you spend a lot of time at home with his work because he knows so much. He knows his numbers 1-10.

Mr. Jon: He knows 1-100 if he is asked.

After completing Raji's progress report, Mrs. Starr handed the Jons a sheet which contained the information she had explained to them.

Mrs. Starr: Do you have any questions?

Mr. Jon: We are going to India to visit family. I will go for two weeks and return to my job, but my wife, Raji and his sister will spend two months there. I asked you to prepare work for him so he will not be behind in his class when he returns. My wife will work with him every day.

Mrs. Starr: Yes, I prepared a packet of material for Raji. I have included a list of children's books to read. He needs to study word families and sight words and sounds. Raji should write a sentence each day. Don't worry about his spelling. If he studies what I have given you, he will be able to catch up when he returns.

[Mrs. Starr quickly thumbed through the materials.]

Mrs. Jon: I would like the books on the list.

Mrs. Starr: Oh no! I can't give them to you. We don't have enough copies, but you might find them in the public library. Oh! Dear! It's time for my next conference. Good luck! Enjoy your trip! If Raji spends time every day on the packets, he may not miss too much. We'll try to catch him up with the class when he returns.

The Jons thanked Mrs. Starr, left the room, and had not explained their visit to India. They believed the trip to India would be an excellent experience for Raji. He would become reacquainted with his relatives and learn about the country. Mrs. Starr didn't ask about their trip. Her major concern was Raji missing two months of school. The parents were also concerned about his schooling, but they believed the trip was an important educational as well as family experience for Raji.

The fall parent conference also caused a communication struggle for Peley's parents. Mrs. Starr attempted to schedule a conference, but they did not appear. She had sent a note home with the date and time, but the parents did not respond. Then she tried calling the home and finally scheduled a conference with Peley's mother. On the day of the conference, Mr. Lom came an hour late. He walked into the room and attempted to talk with Mrs. Starr while she was conferring with another parent. Mrs. Starr stated with exasperation, "Mr. Lom, you are late. I cannot see you now. I am talking with other parents. I will send you the conference papers. If you or your wife have questions, you can contact me." She handed Mr. Lom the papers; he bowed slightly, smiled and left. Mrs. Starr again was startled with this encounter. Later in the day, she told the other teachers, "I don't understand how he could get so messed up. He just doesn't understand!"

During that week, Mr. Lom brought back the papers and information. He clarified, "Better to send home. I work night. Wife work day." When Mrs. Starr asked if he had questions, he said, "No." Mrs. Starr was pleased that they had finally worked out the parent conference, but no conferences, scheduled or unscheduled, occurred that year.

Peley's parents and Raji's parents wanted to communicate with the school, but language and understanding of the school made connections difficult. Mrs. Starr expressed her feelings about communication with the parents, "It's so hard to get them to understand. It's a shame. I wish I could talk with them."

Kid Sheets. Kid Sheets were another means for encouraging home and school communication. During the first month of school, these literacy learning activities were sent home for parent and child to complete together. Mrs. Starr expected them to be returned weekly by each child and shared with the class. Peley never returned the sheets. Raji and his parents completed them; he brought them to class. He was never asked to share them with the class; he never volunteered. Mrs. Starr kept a record of completed and returned sheets and reported that the majority of children and parents were consistent in this exercise. She occasionally asked, "Peley, where are your Kid Sheets? You have not returned them." Peley would respond, "I don't know." Mrs. Starr concluded, "I don't think they understand the purpose of these sheets." Kid Sheets did not seem to help home and school communication with Peley's and Raji's families.

Special school activities. Special school activities were created and designed to specifically involve parents in school to strengthen home and school communication. Raji's parents came to school for most of the daytime and evening activities. Mrs. Jon brought in cupcakes for Raji's birthday, but was not one of the corps of volunteer mothers who helped teachers in class activities. Peley's father was available during the day, but attended few of the functions. However, Mrs. Starr happily reported in December that Mr. Lom was really making an effort.

> Peley's father even came to the Christmas Shop. The parent organization sells used things in good shape and new items such as hats and mittens. He shopped with Peley! He's really trying!

Peley's grandmother and father also attended kindergarten graduation. Mrs. Starr believed that their attendance was a sign of their interest in the school and their children. She considered the attendance factor directly related to home and school communication.

However, Peley's and Raji's families did not find it easy to attend these special occasions. They did not socialize with any other families in the classroom. They came late and stood in a corner talking softly with their child. Peley's grandmother brought graham crackers to share at the graduation party, because she saw the word "refreshments" on the invitation. The efforts to attend these special school activities seemed difficult for both families because they did not know how to communicate effectively with the school. Their struggles were revealed during special school functions because of misunderstanding and lack of communication.

Staff Perceptions and Communication

Staff perceptions of the children's behaviors, socialization and small group interactions were negative, but the staff failed to inform the families.

Perceptions of the children. School staff's communication with the two children's families was strained at times and nonexistent at others. While other children's families were contacted when the staff perceived social, emotional, or academic problems, Peley's and Raji's parents were not notified.

The staff thought Peley was a difficult child, prone to emotional outbursts. Mrs. Starr reported her behaviors in the fall.

She doesn't have a friend, but she's always trying to please me. She tries to be so perfect. She loves responsibilities. Any job or errand is done perfectly without a word said. She concentrates on the work to be done for me. Sometimes, I think she'd like to explode.

Another kindergarten teacher commented, "Peley is so strong willed and when you think you know her, she separates herself from you. She can't stand any criticism no matter how small."

An incident demonstrating staff perceptions occurred one day when Peley returned late from the ESL class. She went to the art center and began coloring a ditto. A teaching assistant asked, "Peley, have you done your apple painting?" Peley kept coloring and replied without looking at the assistant, "I finished it yesterday!" The assistant continued, "But Peley, yesterday was Sunday. We didn't have school. You have to do your apple painting." Peley responded, "I did it!" Then the assistant calmly spoke, "Well let's look for it." Peley emphatically stated, "NO! I'm working." The teacher heard the commotion and came to the situation. The two grimaced and the assistant questioned, "Does she get away with this at home?"

Another incident which caused negative staff perceptions occurred on the pumpkin farm field trip. When Peley went into the barn at the farm, she began complaining about the smell. She bent over the floor and started retching and yelling, "Yuck, the smell makes me sick. I'm damn sick. My mother told me it smells." Mrs. Starr came to rescue her and offered gum to chew. Peley put the gum in her mouth and began to lift her head. Mrs. Starr questioned, "Now what did your mother tell you? What would make you sick, here?" Peley replied, "This place is yuck! I hate the smell!"

The staff was annoyed with her behavior. Mrs. Krupps, another kindergarten teacher, who had taught Peley's brother remarked, "Peley would come to school with the parents when I had her brother. She'd be totally out of control, running wildly around the room. Peley likes being the center of things."

The ESL teacher, Mrs. Brown, also had negative perceptions.

Peley's brother is very different from her. He's calm and quiet. He writes every day in his classroom about how he dislikes his sister. She's a tyrant at home too.

The staff's negative perceptions began to develop when they noticed that Peley often appeared tired in the mornings and complained, "Johnny stayed in the tub too long. We couldn't get him up in the morning. We were late!" She also revealed, "I couldn't get to sleep. My father blew smoke in my face." The staff also concluded that her midmorning aches might be due to an empty stomach. She never ate breakfast at school and said she didn't want it. She also said she didn't want to eat it at home. The staff was puzzled by her stories, but did not contact her family.

Mrs. Starr echoed the perceptions of many staff members when they spoke of Raji.

> I wish I could reach Raji. He always seems so distant; he doesn't speak up in class. I see him as a brilliant little boy who stands back and watches and figures everything out. I worried about him all year, because I didn't see him with a friend.

Mrs. Gerard, the writing-to-read teaching assistant, had little understanding of Raji. She appeared frustrated because he was different. She tried to pronounce his name on the class list and asked, "How do you say your name?" Raji replied quietly saying his first name only. Mrs. Gerard continued, "Whew, that's a tough one. You'll have to help me with your name!" As the weeks went on, she noticed that he was having language problems. "He tries to describe something and he doesn't quite know the names for it."

Mrs. Starr also added concerns about his language,

> When I asked him about the fire trucks we saw at the fire station on our field trip, he didn't seem to be able to tell me about the ladders, poles, or hoses. It was like he didn't understand the whole idea of firetrucks in a fire station.

The other teaching assistant, Mrs. Phazer commented, "I think he has a word retrieval problem. He can't seem to label common nouns."

Unfortunately, the school staff's perceptions of the children did not seem to promote home and school communication with the children's families.

Perceptions of social interactions. The kindergarten staff was concerned about Raji's and Peley's social interactions, but this was never discussed with the parents. They saw atypical dress and lack of friends as examples.

Peley's and Raji's dress was not typical for this kindergarten classroom. Most of the children wore miniature versions of adult fashions along with clothing based on popular television and movie characters. The girls paraded in their lacy leotards and frilly dresses as well as bright-colored stretch pants and oversized sweaters. The boys donned Bugle Boy trousers and the jerseys of national and college athletic teams.

Raji's clothes were usually too small and not the colors or styles commonly worn by the rest of the class. Blacks, reds, and medium blues dominated Raji's wardrobe. Two heavy wool sweaters, tight-fitting corduroy or cotton trousers, socks, and grey and black sneakers with velcro straps were common attire. Mrs. Starr remarked, "He always wears that same blue and red sweater no matter what the temperature indoors or out."

Peley wore tight, ankle high, stone washed jeans, and a turtle-neck, long-sleeved, cotton-knit, sweater with a purple belt. She was the only child with pierced ears and wearing gold earrings. Her long, black, silky, braided pony tail was held with unusual plastic glittery, bowlike clasps. When her sneakers became ragged and dirty, she inherited the saddle shoes her brother had incorrectly chosen. He discovered his mistake when he wore them to school and he became the class target. "Boys don't wear those kind of shoes. Those are girl shoes."

Mrs. Starr commented on Peley's clothing. She recalled the day the class photos were taken.

> Peley came to school dressed as a pink satin and lacy princess. It was the only time she ever wore the dress in school. It had puffed sleeves and a full skirt. She wore a pink ribbon in her pony tail. We called her our princess that day.

Peley's mother said the outfit had been sent to Peley from her Aunt in California. After that day, Peley went back to wearing her same few outfits. During May she acquired a few new fashions. These were simple, short, linenlike dresses with imitation gold jewelry. Her black, torn flats emphasized her bulging feet in white patched stockings. She would come into class in the morning and show Mrs. Starr her new outfit. Mrs. Starr would respond with, "Peley, you look pretty! What a nice outfit!" Peley would then confidently strut to her seat on the rug. A self-satisfied little smile brightened her face.

Since Peley's and Raji's clothing was considered different from their classmates, the staff believed it could have affected social interactions. Additionally, the teachers guessed that their personalities may have contributed to lack of friends. Neither child seemed to have consistent companions throughout the school year.

Mrs. Starr became puzzled about Raji's social interactions when he returned from India. For the first few weeks after his return, he was boisterous, verbal, and friendly. He talked with the other children, asked questions, and laughed aloud. He expressed his ideas. "I like that! That's funny!" Why did you do that?" However, within two weeks, Mrs. Starr observed, "He went back into his shell." He stopped contributing to class discussions and talking to the other children. Mrs. Starr couldn't understand Raji's changes. She didn't communicate with his parents concerning these behaviors.

Peley began the school year unable to make a friend. She was critical of other students and their work. They avoided her or spoke harshly to her. By December, Peley became friendly with Annie and wanted to call her on the phone; Mrs. Starr helped Peley get Annie's phone number. Mrs. Starr also noticed that the kindergarten children invited friends to their homes, but saw no such exchanges between Peley and the other children. Mrs. Starr did not communicate with Peley's family about school friendships.

Perceptions of small group interactions. Observations of social interactions in the small groups revealed that Peley and Raji received negative responses from the children. Mrs. Starr and other staff members were aware of occasional disruptions, but were totally unaware of the frequency and types of negative responses. In any event, the children's social interactions were not discussed with the parents. The following portions of dialogue excerpted in May and June were typical throughout the school year.

At the sand and water table, Raji began to take a plastic boat apart.

> Brian: Don't break it!
> Raji: You can take it apart. It goes back.
> James: [looking at Raji.] You're a troublemaker. You cause trouble. You're a problem!

Raji moved to the corner of the table and left the boat behind. Brian began to take the boat apart while Annie and James watched. No comments were made. Mrs. Starr noticed Raji in the corner, but she did not know what had taken place.

Another example occurred after reading group. Mrs. Starr discovered that Raji could identify all of the pictures of dinosaurs at the discovery table. She asked if he would help some of the children make dinosaur wheels, a circular ditto cutout which depicted the most common dinosaurs. Raji began cutting his and then looked at Jimmy who was cutting spokes in the wheel incorrectly.

Raji: [quietly spoken] You don't cut it like that, like this.
[Raji showed his to Jimmy.].
Billy: [Immediate response in low harsh tones.] I'll pull down your pants.
[Raji backed away as Jimmy faked poking him with scissors.
Annie: [showing Jimmy] Jimmy, Look, it's this way. You're doing it wrong.
Billy: [calmly] Okay. Good.

Billy followed Annie's model. Raji stayed to himself during the rest of the activity not speaking to anyone. Again Mrs. Starr saw Raji move off to the side, but she did not know why.

Peley also had problems with social interactions, but she seemed to initiate the negative. In the block center, she usually made herself boss. "I am the boss. I am strong. I beat my brother!" When it was time to pick up, she would skip off to the bathroom. The other children would comment. "We do all the work. She's a mean boss."

One day in May, while at the writing/drawing table, Peley began wiggling her front bottom tooth.

Peley: See my tooth! I pulled my tooth and it hurt. I threw it away. My brother threw all his away in the trash.
Jonny: No you don't do that! It's for the tooth fairy. You put your tooth under the pillow and the tooth fairy brings you money!
Peley: No it don't!
Annie: My mother put five dollars under my pillow.
Linda: It was the tooth fairy. She puts the money there. She puts the money and takes the tooth to keep.
Peley: No, it hurts! You throw it in the trash. I know!

The conversation ended when the teaching assistant arrived to show the children how to play the Yak Game in the readiness center. In both scenes, Peley could not interact appropriately. She didn't understand how to be a leader without making the children angry. She also did not understand the meaning of the "tooth fairy," thus isolating herself from relevant conversation with her classmates.

Summary of Home and School Communication

Normally, there was strong home and school communication between the kindergarten families and the school, but the school did not effectively communicate with either Peley's or Raji's families. The families did not effectively communicate with the school. This lack of communication created cultural conflict and left the children's visible struggles unattended.

Mrs. Starr and the parents expected the ESL program to assist literacy learning and help the children fit into the kindergarten program. However, when Peley and Raji began to have difficulties, explorations of causation did not occur. There were no questions about home language, customs, literature, and values. Peley's and Raji's families were simply expected to understand and participate.

Peley's and Raji's families did not feel comfortable communicating with the school. Their difficulties were manifested in their understanding of the ESL program and the children's social interactions. Both familes saw the ESL class as important to the children's literacy learning. Even though Peley's parents knew she did not like going, they believed it was necessary for her academic progress. Raji's parents thought ESL class was important until they discovered that Raji had been leaving the reading group to go to ESL twice a week. They believed Raji should not miss classes, but they did not question the school.

Similarly, social interactions were not addressed by the families. Peley's mother knew Peley wanted a friend from school, but her mother did not know how to help her. She did not communicate these concerns to the school. Similarly, Raji returned from India as a boisterous, verbal child, but after several weeks withdrew to himself. His parents were concerned, but did not communicate with the school.

Language in written and oral communication seemed to hinder connections with the children's parents. Mrs. Starr did not communicate her concerns to the parents, because she believed they might not understand. She had an especially difficult time communicating with Peley's parents, since she believed their English was so limited.

While other children's parents were contacted when the staff perceived problems during the school year, Peley's and Raji's were not. At the end of the year, Mrs. Starr invited Raji's family for a conference. She recommended that Raji attend the summer literacy maintenance program. She told them that his reading test scores, his work in the writing-to-read program, the ESL language assessment and his socialization in the classroom demonstrated a need for practicing his English literacy learning during the summer. The parents were also surprised to learn that Raji had been leaving reading group to go to ESL class. They agreed to send Raji to the summer program, which meant canceling his registration in a summer day camp. Raji's parents were not happy about the lack of school communication. They made the decision then that they would not allow Raji to go to ESL in first grade unless it was an after school program. They believed Raji's literacy suffered due to the ESL pull-out. They did not inform the school of their decision at that time.

Mrs. Starr did not communicate with Peley's parents at the end of the year. She explained to Peley that she should read books over the summer and suggested that she attend a community day camp.

The school's stance was in contrast with current research which exhorts educators to communicate and connect with the home cultures for the development of successful English literacy learning (Cummins, 1986; Levine, 1987; Reyhner & Garcia, 1989; Trueba, et al., 1990; Dyson, 1993). Schools across our nation face similar dilemmas with their language-minority children when they adopt an assimilationist perspective (Banks, 1997). Additionally, White middle class teachers have often lived lives isolated from diverse groups of people and do not understand the need to become aware and respond sensitively to minority children (Pattniak, 1996; Schmidt, 1996a). Therefore, the next chapter will offer an array of ideas and strategies for present and future teachers as they attempt to celebrate diversity in their classrooms and schools.

Since early childhood programs frequently emphasize learning about the seasons with related holidays, it is quite natural to fit global celebrations into the present school curriculum.

Classroom Community: Diversity and Literacy

This story is about a kindergarten classroom community where Peley and Raji, two language-minority children, struggled to develop their English literacy. Over the years, we have learned that many factors outside the classroom influence literacy learning, such as the children's home culture, socioeconomic level, cognitive abilities, and emotional characteristics, but I believe Peley and Raji had to deal with a set of problems unique to language-minority children in our nation. Their home cultures and language differed from the school culture, and their teachers and parents were unable to help them reconcile and celebrate differences. Similar to the African American children in Rist's study, *The Invisible Children* (1978), Peley and Raji were invisible when they blended into the classroom culture, working and playing without incident. However, they were visible problems when their struggles became obvious in the dominant White classroom culture. Also, similar to the teacher in Kidder's study, *Among Schoolchildren* (1989), Mrs. Starr struggled. She had always lived and worked in European American cultural settings and had not been trained to assist language-minority children's literacy development. She presumed that the school ESL program would provide for their learning needs.

So, when Peley and Raji entered her classroom, Mrs. Starr expected them to assimilate in the tradition of the Melting Pot image. When they began to struggle, she attempted strategies learned in her teacher preparation programs and previous classroom experiences. When these proved futile, she guessed that the children might need a little more time to fit in. Furthermore, since Mrs. Starr had morning and afternoon kindergartens totaling more than forty children, the demands of the daily school schedule gave her little time to think specifically about the two children. She knew that Peley's and Raji's home languages and customs were different, but she was confused and could not connect with the families. She did not communicate as frequently with their families as she did with others, because she feared they would not understand. Consequently, cultural conflict was inevitable.

What I discovered during my year of observations in this kindergarten program was not unusual. Many researchers suggest that language-minority children have great difficulty fitting into the context of classrooms in the United States (Au & Mason, 1981; Hakuta, 1986; Trueba, et al., 1990). Their struggles are believed to occur because they must function within at least two cultures, home and school, as they develop their English literacy. It is also believed that the moment language-minority children begin to read and write in the dominant language, the cultures of their homes affect their success or failure in the school culture (Wong-Filmore, 1983; VerHoeven,1987; Swain, 1988; Reyhner & Garcia, 1989; Trueba, et al., 1990). Therefore, the sociocultural perspective which views the literacy learning process as social and cultural (Heath, 1983; Taylor, 1983; Schieffelin & Cochran-Smith, 1984; Taylor & Dorsey-Gaines; 1988; Moll, 1990) was adopted as the guiding perspective for observing Peley and Raji. In this kindergarten, literacy learning was viewed as a social phenomenon; thus ethnography provided the means for examining the children's learning. I described the teacher's struggles and the children's struggles during work and play settings, formal literacy learning and classroom celebrations. Finally, I examined home and school communication related to the two children (1993a).

What I learned from the year of exploration and observation contributes to our understanding of cultural conflict and struggle in similar kindergarten and early childhood programs. Issues were raised which support specific suggestions for the development of literacy learning in classroom communities that include language-minority children. Most suggestions will require varying amounts of teacher time for research and study. As with any new curriculum ideas, carefully attentive implementation and assessment of student responses are important (DeCorse, 1996; Xu, 1996). Hopefully, teacher motivation and school district understanding and appreciation will serve as the means to initiate, develop, and establish multicultural settings.

Work and Play Suggestions

Peley and Raji were visibly different. The two children dressed in clothing not typical in color, style or fit. Their brown skin, brown eyes, and black hair were unusual in the blond, blue-eyed school. Their dress and physical appearance may have motivated the discrimination they experienced during work and play settings, since it has been reported that children by age four have developed racist views through the media as well as through the dominant community culture (Blanchard, 1983; Milner, 1983; Derman-Sparks, 1992). Often schools unknowingly contribute to these attitudes by ignoring differences. Educators may even believe that color blindness is the way to teach tolerance (Jackson & Cosca, 1974; Milner, 1983; Powell, 1983). However, it is recommended that acknowledging and celebrating differences helps to eliminate stereotyping in classrooms (Ogbu, 1986; Gougis, 1986; Ortiz, 1988; Cummins, 1989; Percell, 1989). Schools must deliberately provide opportunities for all students to learn about and respect diversity.

Teachers who help their children appreciate diversity and understand the realities of discrimination can create antiracist, multicultural settings (Nieto, 1996). Appreciating similarities and differences in the world around us is an important first step in the creation of inclusive social settings (Banks, 1997).

Similarities and differences. Since the study of colors is part of kindergarten programs, a daily celebration of our colorful world is a natural means for observing similarities and differences among people, places and things. When the kindergarten children drew pictures of themselves at the beginning of the school year, Raji depicted himself as a brown muscle man and Peley portrayed herself as the elegant Asian lady in the long green gown. When children draw themselves, this is a natural means for class discussions about how we are alike and different. Multicultural crayons or paints also allow children to experiment with color and observe similarities and differences in skin tones.

Similarities and differences in music, clothing, food, family, customs, entertainment, and language may be explored weekly at a learning center and during whole group activities. A world globe at one of the centers would serve to stimulate questions and comments. Sharing food from around the world during snack time is a way to taste similarities and differences. Lively discussions of similarities and differences among the children during share time each day would provide opportunities for literacy learning as community. The following are suggested activities for centers that serve to increase knowledge and assist in learning to value similarities and differences:

1. The discovery learning center might include a globe and be a place to observe similar and different facial features around the world.
2. The block center may be a place to build houses from around the world and discuss similar and different shapes and materials.
3. The listening center could include songs from around the world to sing. Children could learn the functions of music in various cultures.
4. The housekeeping center would be a place to dress in clothing from around the world and feel its use and style.
5. The readiness center might have games from around the world to connect with fun in other cultures.
6. The writing center may depict vocabulary from around the world, giving children familiar pictures, words and symbols related to English.
7. The math center could be a place where the universality of number concepts might be shared as well as number words in different languages.
8. The library center would include literature about other places and cultures.
9. The sand and water center might provide activities for the study of geography.

If these centers had existed at East Side Elementary, Peley might have shared her Vietnamese and Cambodian hair clasps and other pieces of jewelry. Raji might have explained his family celebrations and spoken about his two months in India.

Inclusive social settings. Negative social interactions throughout the school year prevented positive experiences for the two children as well as their classmates. Peley usually attempted to dominate and was critical of students working or playing around her. Raji usually kept to himself in small groups. When he did attempt to join in an activity, he was usually rebuffed. Mrs. Starr changed their groups, allowed them choice, and attempted to pair both children with a variety of other children in the classroom, but to no avail.

Celebrating human similarities and differences is a natural lead into social interactions. Peley and Raji were not accepted because of their differences. If they had felt comfortable about sharing their languages and cultures, and if their classmates had been prepared to appreciate differences, many of the negative exchanges might not have occurred. When children see, hear, taste, touch, and experience differences on a daily basis, they will become accustomed to differences and realize the rewards.

The suggested activities relating to similarities and differences are initial ideas that can be gradually adopted and adapted as teachers become more comfortable with children's responses. The only caveat for attempting these activities is to remember that when teachers avoid discussing differences, discrimination is allowed to continue without question, thus perpetuating racist attitudes.

Formal Literacy Learning Suggestions

This kindergarten's formal literacy program appeared to be based on the interactive perspective (Rumelhart & McClelland, 1986; Pearson, et. al., 1991). Usually, student prior knowledge was connected to phonological awareness, basic print awareness, word awareness and letter recognition, for successful beginning reading (Adams, 1991). The components of this program were learning centers, a literature-based reading series, and a language program with an additional computer-assisted, writing-to-read lab (Martin, 1984). Peley and Raji were in the top reading group for the formal program and were pulled out of the group for two days a week to attend the ESL program. Peley was reading independently by January. Raji remained in the top reading group even after being in India for two months of the school year. However, both children often seemed distracted and uninvolved during lessons and their social relationships suffered. Multicultural materials, an inclusive ESL program and relevant assessment procedures are suggestions that could be implemented in early childhood programs similar to East Side Elementary School's Kindergarten Program.

Multicultural Materials. A lack of culturally related materials may have contributed to the negative behaviors found in the kindergarten program at East Side Elementary School. The literature-based series included a multicultural strand, but it was not used. There were no maps, videos, or artifacts related to Southeast Asia or India. Peley's favorite books were Dr. Seuss, whose creatures were comical and culturally neutral. Raji's favorite book was a *A Snowy Day* (1962), by Ezra Jack Keats, the story of an African American boy whose skin tone matched Raji's.

Numerous studies demonstrate that when language-minority children's cultures are ignored, they often become disinterested in school. It is important for the children to see some connections with their own cultures for effective English literacy learning (Cummins, 1986; Moll, 1990; Trueba, et al., 1990). Similarly, just as teachers typically help European American students connect the "known to the new" (Herber & Herber 1993), they also must draw upon the prior knowledge of language-minority children.

Multicultural literature and materials can provide the means for helping language-minority children connect their home cultures with the school culture for English literacy learning. When literature from a child's culture is part of the school program, the child's home language and culture are validated (Rasinski & Padak, 1990). Additionally, these materials will help develop classmates' understanding and appreciation of the language-minority culture, thus assisting in the development of community (Cummins, 1986; Early, 1990; Dyson, 1993).

Suggestions for this program and others like it would include the use of multicultural literature and materials that reflect not only the cultures in the classroom, but other cultures around the world. The following may help:

1. In consultation with families, the school librarian and other teachers, materials could be explored and shared on a daily basis (Reyhner & Garcia, 1989).
2. Videos about other places and faces spark children's interest and create opportunities for questions and comments.
3. Annotated reference lists of multicultural children's literature exist in teacher magazines, especially *The Reading Teacher* and *Language Arts* so teachers can select appropriate books for their classrooms and schools.
4. Literature activities in library corners and listening centers help children become familiar with other cultures.
5. Daily read-alouds, typical in early childhood classrooms, provide the means for studying multicultural literature.
6. Encouraging children to share similarities and difference during reading, writing, listening, and talking about the literature of their culture and others enhances the multicultural literacy learning setting (Au, 1993; Battle, 1993).
7. Children may explore storytelling and recitation of poetry, reader's theater, reenactment of significant national and world events, and dramatization of famous national and world people. These are valuable literacy activities often practiced in other cultures, but frequently neglected in our own (Heath, 1983; Igoa, 1995).

8. Children could regularly share their home languages with the class, encouraging classmates to learn other languages (Barone, 1996). Picture/word cards with English and another language help children develop an interest in other cultures.

Peley may have written stories about visiting with her cousins on weekends or celebrating Tet, the Vietnamese New Year. Raji may have written about his family in India, Indian thanksgiving celebration and other holidays. The above activities might have helped in connecting home and school cultures and assisted in building classroom respect for diversity (Feeley, 1983).

Many more activities can be created and developed by present and future teachers when they have opportunities to systematically study other cultures and discover the wealth of stories and materials that lend themselves to an understanding and appreciation of diversity.

ESL Program. Typical of ESL pull-out programs across the United States, the East Side Elementary ESL program seemed to stigmatize the children and cause discontinuity in learning (Skutnabb-Kangas & Cummins, 1988; McKay, 1988; Moll, 1992). Peley and Raji lacked continuity in reading group stories and lessons, because they left the reading group two days a week for the ESL class; there was no planned lesson coordination between the two teachers. Peley initially resisted leaving the kindergarten classroom, but went willingly when she was allowed to occasionally bring a friend. Mrs. Starr didn't want the children leaving reading group and often wondered what they were learning in the ESL class.

An ESL program coordinated with the classroom program negates exclusion. But the ESL teacher and classroom teacher must have time in their schedules to plan and coordinate for classroom inclusion (McKay, 1988; Moll, 1990). If Mrs. Brown and Mrs. Starr had had the time to plan together, Mrs. Brown might have been able to work with Peley and Raji in the reading group and even assist other children at the same time. Mrs. Brown might have occasionally worked outside the classroom with Peley and Raji, but could have coordinated her lessons with Mrs. Starr. Also, Mrs. Brown could have presented lessons about other cultures to the whole kindergarten. These activities would have made her a familiar teacher for all the children rather than the person who took Peley and Raji out of the classroom social setting. Such a arrangement in this classroom and similar classrooms allows the whole class to benefit from another teacher and program and negates the potential isolation of language-minority children. Discontinuity and stigmatization may be avoided in early childhood inclusive ESL programs.

Assessment. The findings from this examination of two language-minority children in a kindergarten program imply that there should be multiple strategies for literacy assessment, since cultural biases of the test and the tester may influence evaluations and interpretations (Hakuta, 1986; Stuckey, 1991).

Peley and Raji were in the highest reading ability group in the kindergarten. Even though native languages were spoken in the homes of both children, their parents emphasized learning to read and write English. Both children read and wrote stories in English at home. Nevertheless, when the staff assessed their literacy development, they were concerned with the maintenance of literacy learning and the development of socialization skills.

Formal tests of the children's reading and writing indicated difficulties with sequence, vocabulary development, and idioms. Mrs. Starr also thought oral and written expression were sometimes problematic for both children, but especially for Raji. She was not confident about their literacy development. Additionally, Mrs. Brown's interpretation of the language assessment test given at the end of the year indicated that both children needed to continue ESL classes in first grade.

At the same time, the building reading teacher reported that Peley had almost scored high enough to be in the first grade intellectually gifted program, but she was not recommended. No one in the school was aware of cultural bias and its influence on evaluations. Peley was placed in an above average reading group for first grade and encouraged to regularly visit the public library for reading practice during the summer months. Mrs. Starr, in the hopes of improving Peley's social skills, told the child about summer day camp in her neighborhood. The staff informed Raji's parents that he would be placed in an average ability, first grade reading group. They also strongly suggested that Raji attend the summer school literacy maintenance program for academic as well as social skills.

Assessment of literacy learning in multicultural settings must be carefully considered. Educators interpret test results without thinking about existing cultural biases. They do not recognize that many tests do not actually inform us of the language abilities of language-minority students (Figueroa, 1989). Cultural bias is present in standardized tests (Hakuta, 1986), an English language power relationship exists between tester and testee (Delgado-Gaitan, 1989; Schuerich, 1993) and standard English proficiency acts as a prerequisite rather than a goal when interpreting the tests (Rigg & Allen, 1989). Furthermore, negative teacher attitudes about second language students may add to assessment problems (Piestrup, 1973).

Suggestions for kindergarten and early childhood programs would include staff scrutiny of assessment procedures and staff study of authentic ways to evaluate second language learning (Crowell, Kawakami & Wong, 1986). When reading materials and writing assignments are culturally relevant and familiar, language-minority children's performance is significantly higher (Reyhner & Garcia, 1989). Families may be capable of helping teachers create and develop reading and writing materials and assignments that connect home and school for literacy learning through explanations of family stories, customs and entertainment (Faltis, 1993). Student performance and responses may then more accurately reflect their growth and development for evaluations of their English literacy learning (McCaleb, 1994; Schmidt, 1996a). Staff assessment must always weigh the importance of cultural influences when recommendations are made for future placements.

Holidays and Celebration Suggestions

The descriptions of this kindergarten classroom during holidays and celebrations imply that schools must become aware of the increasingly diverse populations in their classrooms. Often the dominant cultural holidays and celebrations found in schools are exclusively emphasized without considering other minority cultures. When students are given the message that they must assimilate at the expense of their home cultures, it appears that their learning suffers (Cummins, 1989; Trueba, et al., 1990; Snow, 1992). Therefore, it is suggested that present and future teachers connect home and school cultures for language-minority children's literacy development (Heath, 1983; Delgado-Gaitian, 1989; Hatton, 1989; Dyson, 1993).

Peley and Raji visibly struggled in the classroom during most holidays and classroom celebrations. They attempted to fit in but they were usually confused. The community where they lived was overwhelmingly white, blue collar, and Roman Catholic. Explaining appropriate costumes, colors, and traditional behaviors was not considered necessary in the kindergarten program. Peley's mother said they were Christians, but Christmas decorations or celebrations were not in the home. They did not exchange presents, so Peley did not understand the meaning of making white paste imprints of her hands as gifts for her parents. Raji did not realize the significance of wearing green on St. Patrick's Day. Both children were confused by Easter. Peley drew red and green rabbits. Raji typed a story, "the rabit is sile bekos it is fall." When asked to tell about the rabbit, Raji explained, "He eats too much eggs."

Peley had greater difficulties with classroom festivities than Raji. The reasons may be that Raji's father had earned one of his degrees from a university in the United States. The family also had regular contact with the school district's family literacy program. Their spoken English was grammatically correct with almost perfect enunciation. In contrast, Peley's parents had the equivalent of an elementary education in Cambodia and Vietnam. They worked day and night shifts, preventing them from being actively involved in the school program. It was also difficult to understand their spoken English.

Peley and Raji were not asked about holidays or celebrations unique to their homes, but neither were any of the other children. It was assumed that all in the class were celebrating similarly. Because holidays and celebrations were an integral part of the kindergarten curriculum, Peley and Raji were immediately placed at a disadvantage. They experienced cultural conflict as they visibly struggled to understand. The study of culturegrams and the inclusion of celebrations and customs around the world can alleviate cultural struggles and create an appreciation for differences.

Culturegrams. Culturegrams, published by some state education departments around the country, include activities for holidays and celebrations from many cultures around the world. The activities help language-minority children as well as their classmates understand the form and function of these special times (Igoa, 1995). Ideas for effective communication with language-minority families and reference lists for teacher research of cultures are also included. After reading them, it becomes clear that people throughout the world have similar holidays related to the seasons of the year (Dresser, 1994).

Seasons and Holidays. Since early childhood programs frequently emphasize learning about the seasons with related holidays, it is quite natural to fit global celebrations into the present school curriculum. New year holidays of renewal, winter holidays of light, spring holidays of rebirth, harvest holidays of thanksgiving and summer days of communal games and activities can include Tet, Chinese New Year, Hanukkah, Christmas, Kwanza, Easter, and many more. None are excluded while children become familiar with global celebrations and learn to embrace the joy and wonder experienced by people around the world who participate in them. Costumes, games, music, dance, food, rituals, and stories can be studied and shared. Thus an early childhood classroom may begin to prepare children to become confident contributing members in a classroom community, so that in the future they may become active members in the global community (Dresser, 1994).

Home and School Communication Suggestions

Home and school connections are key components of literacy learning for language-minority children (Au & Mason, 1981; Reyhner & Garcia, 1989; Quintero & Huerta-Macias, 1990; Goldenberg, 1990; Edwards, 1996). Au (1993) recommends frequent parent meetings and parent participation in the classroom for the prevention of cultural conflict. The two children's cultural struggles were manifested in their social interactions, literacy learning, and understanding of holidays and celebrations. If home and school communication had been strong, the conflicts may not have existed. However, the weak home and school communication itself may have been a symptom of cultural conflict (Jacob & Sanday, 1976).

Research supports the idea that parents of language-minority students are genuinely interested in their children's schooling and want the children to fit into the program (Clay, 1976), but poor communication with the teacher and lack of understanding of family values prevents their involvement (Wong-Filmore, 1983; Moll & Diaz, 1987; Delgado-Gaitian, 1989; Olson, 1990; Ballinger, 1992; Tan, 1992). Therefore, the school must reach out to the parents for effective communication (Ogbu, 1983). Similarly, the parents in this study seemed to want their children to fit into the school culture, but they did not communicate with the school about their children's programs or progress. The school staff was concerned about Peley and Raji, but did not communciate their concerns to the parents. The teachers may have benefited from regular dialogue with the parents, but communication with the families was considered too difficult.

Suggestions for home and school communication could be

adapted from a series of approaches (Faltis, 1993; Mc Caleb, 1994; Schmidt, 1996a; Edwards, 1996). It is necessary to keep in mind that developing positive home and school communication is a process accomplished in stages for the purpose of developing communication and trust. These suggestions are based on several premises. First, the family and child's home community are the child's first teachers who possess valuable knowledge to contribute to the classroom and school (McCaleb,1994; Edwards, 1996). Second, the school has the responsibility to reach out to families and communities and connect for relevancy in the classroom and school (Heath, 1983); Faltis, 1993; Schmidt, 1996b). Without these basic ideas, home and school communication will be superficial at best. Finally, translators are important people to consult. They not only translate language, but also usually translate culture.

The following stages may be best implemented when the entire school decides to connect with families and community. However, individual teachers and teams may decide to be the initiators or change agents by systematically attempting this sequence on a small scale. Disclaimers for these steps relate to neighborhood safety factors, but violence in our society appears to be an equal opportunity phenomenon. Many of the communities that have been stereotypically labeled as violent are not. But if a lone teacher feels uncomfortable, a community member who works in the school may act as a liason for introduction.

1. First, meeting the families informally in their homes and community establishes interest and trust. When teachers are seen in local stores and neighborhoods, there is a greater likelihood that casual conversation with language-minority families can occur in a relaxed and spontaneous manner. Even when the language is a barrier, pleasant nods and positive greetings can be conveyed with body language and gestures. What's most important is the sincere attempt to communicate. Mistakes are usually overlooked when human kindness and honest interest are involved.

    The following letter and information sheet on the next page may be mailed home or discussed at an informal home or school meeting (Squires, 1993). The letter and form might be translated before it is sent or delivered.

September 1999

Dear Family,

It is our understanding that your child speaks a language other than English. We want your child to share your language while he/she is learning to read, write and speak English in school. We believe that the children in our classroom will benefit from discovering other languages and cultures. We believe this will improve their education and help them understand people. We also invite you to visit our classroom at any time to listen, watch, or help us while we learn.

We have attached pages to this letter which we hope you will complete. If you would like, we will have someone who speaks your language meet with you to gather the information about your country of origin, family, work, celebrations, language, literature, art, music, dance, drama, and games. Soon, I would also like to meet with you in your home and/or in school at your convenience.

Thank you for helping us with your child's education.

Sincerely yours,

Please Tell Us About Your..........

Family	Language	Literature
Homes	Vocabulary	Folktales/stories
Clothing	Phrases/idioms	Illustrators/artists
Food	Symbols/Letters	Proverbs
Care of children	Numbers	Poetry
Transportation		
School	Work	Nature/Homeland
		Animals
Art	Technology	Plants
Jewelry		Geography
Carving		
Sculpting	Music/Dance	Games
Painting	Instruments	Indoor
Weaving	Drama	Outdoor

2. The next stage of communication may occur at informal informational meetings about school curriculum, special events, and student progress (Faltis, 1993). These may happen at any time of the day or night in school or in the home since language-minority families often have unusual work schedules, based on available jobs. At these meetings, families may be encouraged to share talents, customs, and work experiences at a future time in the classroom. They may be asked to assist with basic classroom tasks, such as guiding on field trips or listening to children read stories.

3. Teachers may also ask to interview families at a future date to discover cultural similarities and differences and ways to work most successfully with their children (Schmidt, 1996b; Edwards, 1996). Before interviews, the teacher may find it helpful to outline key events in his or her own life in order to honestly see cultural similarities and differences when completing family interviews. This can serve as a check on the problems associated with ethnocentricism (Spindler & Spindler, 1987). The following procedure, known as the ABC's of cross-cultural communication (Schmidt, 1996b), helps teachers understand and appreciate cultural differences which may cause discomfort and conflict:

(a) Write your autobiography, beginning with your earliest memories. Try to remember and list significant events in your life. The more details you can remember, the more useful your cross-cultural analyses of children and their families.

(b) Using unstructured interview procedures, ask families to tell about early school and home experiences in their own lives. For instance, "Tell me about your first school and teachers or tell me about your home when you were a child." Allow families to share their stories in detail. A teacher may meet several times with a family in order to get as many details as possible. Even if families are in the earliest stages of learning English, they will tell you valuable information about the past that helps in understanding the present. If the past is too painful for them to share, they will frequently want to talk about their adjustments to new places and faces.

(c) Next the teacher makes a list of similarities and differences between his or her own life story and the interviewee's story. From this list the analyses of differences is important.

(d) When analyzing the differences, think about what differences make you uncomfortable and why. Additionally, what differences do you find appealing and why. Allow your mind to wonder why your culture does not view an issue in the same way.

Completing this exercise helps us gain a healthy respect for differences. When we see that the study of differences broadens our perspectives, the mainstream culture is enriched.

4. The previous stage encourages parent participation and sharing in the classroom. Follow-up invitations with phone calls and letters are a sign that the teacher sincerely wishes that families join the class and share. Some family members may only want to observe and that should also suffice, since the school needs to be a welcoming environment.

5. In the final stage of home and school communication, families are involved in curricular decisions. Student's placements, methods, and materials are discussed and demonstrated to families. Then home literacy learning can be connected to school definitions of literacy learning. Children can see relevancy to their learning. The rest of the class also learns about differences and the power of diverse perspectives (Nieto, 1996). Finally, this stage is meant to empower families by the very nature of their inclusion into the educational community. It allows the child, family, and community opportunities to take control of their own learning for successful transition into the mainstream of society. Furthermore, society benefits from educated, confident new perspectives that breathe new life into the culture of the United States of America.

If Peley's and Raji's parents had been a part of a home and school connection program, cultural conflict and struggles might have been avoided. Even though Raji's family's English was excellent, a translator probably could have helped interpret home and school expectations.

Where Do We Go From Here?

Many of the suggestions for classrooms with language-minority children could be implemented in all classrooms with minor modifications. These ideas not only assist English literacy learning but also help prepare all of our children for the global community. Such preparation is in the best interests of our nation and the planet Earth.

Sadly, this year-long account of a kindergarten implies that schools may actually interfere with children's literacy learning if they do not work to understand the diverse cultural backgrounds of the children in classrooms. Educators often choose to avoid contact with individuals of different cultures. Thus the burden of interpretation of the school culture is placed on language-minority students and their families. Schools must take the first steps toward connecting with the home cultures (Jacob & Sanday, 1976). Students must not be required to sacrifice their cultural heritage in order to achieve success in school (Rodriguez, 1982; Hoffman, 1989; Tan, 1992). Finally, teacher education programs must prepare educators with the means to enhance the literacy learning of language-minority students, the fastest growing school population (Garcia, 1994).

My hope is that readers of this story take the information learned from students and staff at East Side Elementary School Kindergarten and use it to alleviate the struggles for their children and children in similar programs. When Mrs. Starr read about her kindergarten classroom and the struggles of Peley and Raji, she decided to try several suggestions in her classroom the following year. The Epilogue in this book is an enlightening description of her successes and obstacles in the process of advocating for changes in her classroom and school.

Author's note:

Mrs. Starr and I became great friends. We learned many lessons together. I have not personally stayed in contact with Peley, Raji and their families, but plan to reconnect and pursue a study of their education during middle and high school.

The classroom globe became a favorite place to gather in the mornings as students found countries related to the cultures they studied.

8

Epilogue: Teacher as Change Agent

Becoming Aware

Mrs. Starr became aware of the need for multicultural literacy learning when she read about Peley's and Raji's struggles in her classroom (Schmidt, 1993a; 1993b). She responded by studying the literature and outlining a plan to change practice in her own classroom and school. Additionally, she enlisted colleagues who would share in the creation and implementation of a plan. Her reflections during the following school year contribute to our understanding of the change process as well as the teacher as change agent. Even though her project met with conflicts, the strength of the successes provided the impetus to continue (Schmidt, 1996a).

> During this first five years of my teaching career, I noticed that language-minority students usually had emotional problems as well as literacy learning problems in my kindergarten classroom. I believe that my failure to understand and appreciate other cultures affected student classroom behavior and performance.

Mrs. Starr expressed these concerns about her past practices after realizing the importance of multicultural literacy learning in her own classroom and school. Her discovery occurred at the end of the school year when she read descriptions of her classroom setting (Schmidt, 1993a; 1993b). She realized that Peley's and Raji's struggles related to cultural conflicts during formal literacy learning sessions, work and play settings, holidays and classroom celebrations, and home and school communications. Subsequently, Mrs. Starr concluded, "I have to learn how to work effectively with children from other cultures."

As with the teacher in *Among Schoolchildren* (Kidder, 1989), it was not in Mrs. Starr's European American experiences to understand other cultures. Also, her teacher training had not promoted contact and understanding of other cultures. Since she and I had developed a collegial relationship during the previous year of my participant observations and interviews, I gave her a list of references cited in my study. Throughout the following summer, we met several times to discuss the readings. From our sharing, Mrs. Starr formulated ideas for a plan which could bring multicultural literacy learning to her classroom and school. She also informed her advisor in her master of elementary education degree program that she would like to keep a journal during the project and write a paper about her year's work; the advisor granted permission.

Since I saw this as a unique opportunity to observe an empowered teacher researcher on a deliberate course to make change, based on her perceived need for change, I asked if I might record her reflections; she agreed.

Teacher reflections have often given us insights into practice (Schon, 1983; 1987; Elbaz, 1991; Gardner, 1991). Since the promotion of teachers as change agents in classrooms and schools is a phenomenon related to the school restructuring movement (Berends, 1992; Hargreaves, 1996), there is a need to gain information about how individual teachers think as they are involved in a change process in their own classrooms and schools (Atkin, 1991; Fullan & Hargreaves, 1991). I saw the recording of Mrs. Starr's reflections as a means to help us understand her thinking during the first year of implementing her multicultural literacy learning project. I also hoped her thoughts would reveal insights about individual teachers as change agents (Fullan, 1993).

Studying for the Project

In preparation for her project, Mrs. Starr read research which suggests that children who represent language-minority groups have great difficulties fitting into the context of American classrooms (Hakuta, 1986; Trueba, et al., 1990). Their difficulties are often attributed to the assimilationist perspective, which proposes that success in the United States depends on fitting into the economic and social mainstream culture of society (Rist, 1978; Porter, 1990). However, this perspective in education often disempowers students by ignoring or subtracting the home culture (Cardenas, 1977; Cummins, 1989; Treuba, et al.,1990). Consequently, the children's struggles are believed to occur because they need to function within at least two cultures as they develop their literacies (Cummins, 1989; Peter, 1994; Watts Pailliotet, 1994).

Like many educators, Mrs. Starr recalled her own past struggles when working with language-minority children, because of her lack of cultural understanding. She was hesitant about communicating with parents because of a fear that they wouldn't understand. She ignored student differences because of a belief that they needed to blend into the school setting. Subsequently, her perusal of the research revealed that she was not alone in her struggles (Rist, 1973; Ogbu, 1978; Phillips, 1983; Spindler, 1987; Cuban, 1989; Kidder, 1989; Faltis, 1993). She spoke to other educators and found that they had experienced the same difficulties when working with language-minority children. Therefore, as a reflective practitioner (Schon, 1983; 1987) she began sharing information and questions with trusted colleagues.

Mrs. Starr also discovered research which proposed that teacher understanding of students' cultural backgrounds (Ogbu, 1978; Au & Mason, 1981; Phillips, 1983; Spindler, 1987; Divoky, 1988) can help teachers appreciate cultural diversity, which in turn will help students reconcile cultural differences and develop their literacies. Also, teacher attitudes about their own abilities to teach children of diverse backgrounds can affect student literacy learning in classrooms (Good & Brophy, 1991). Moreover, Mrs. Starr found that teacher education programs have only recently begun to prepare teachers for multicultural classrooms (Cummins, 1991; Goodlad, 1991; Nieto, 1996). Consequently, most teachers in the field are often left to their own initiatives to make changes for multicultural education (Trueba, Jacobs & Kirton, 1990; Atkin, 1991; Fullan, 1993). Stimulated by reading, and empowered by a need for change, Mrs. Starr envisioned change in her own classroom and school (Kincheloe & Steinberg, 1993). She hoped that her efforts would be joined by colleagues.

A Positive Start
During the summer, Mrs. Starr presented information about multicultural literacy learning to the principal and described the difficulties encountered by language-minority students in her own classroom and possibly other classrooms in the school. Additionally, she explained the need for change and proposed a plan for change. The principal agreed with her and then outlined what should be included in a project proposal submitted to the school district central administration. Explanations of purpose, rationale and contributions, parent, student, and staff involvement, procedures for implementation, and time factors were required. A week before school began, the proposal was accepted and Mrs. Starr was permitted to proceed.

At a fall faculty meeting, she described her classroom from the previous year and portrayed the struggles of the language minority children and their families. She answered questions from colleagues and asked for a volunteer steering committee who would be willing to examine ways to connect home and school cultures, work more closely with the ESL teacher, gather multicultural literature, and implement multicultural activities in the classroom. Mrs. Starr concluded:

> Through the use of multicultural literature and activities, parent involvement, and teacher-to-teacher communication, we can begin to bring other cultures, new holidays, and new ideas into our classrooms. Children will become aware of differences in people in their community and learn to appreciate those differences.

The following week, two first grade teachers, one second grade teacher, and the ESL teacher volunteered to join the steering committee. They met briefly as a group on Friday and decided to meet after school on a bimonthly schedule. Their objectives were to explore ways to facilitate multicultural literacy learning and develop an appreciation for cultural diversity. Mrs. Starr was pleased with the initial efforts: "This is a great start! I never expected this much interest." Because of her own enthusiasm and study of the literature, she immediately began making changes in her classroom.

Reflections on Changes in Classroom Practice

Mrs. Starr reflected upon her past classroom practice and was determined to make changes:

> Every school year, with the rest of the teachers in our school, I filled my classroom with Columbus, Halloween, Thanksgiving, Christmas, valentines, shamrocks and Easter rabbits with no thoughts of individual children's home celebrations. I believed that these holidays were important to the majority of children; the minority children would eventually understand. I now realize the confusions they might have experienced. I knew I had to make changes in my classroom practice.

Using the materials, discussions, and ideas developed during steering committee meetings, Mrs. Starr attempted to change her classroom lessons to promote multicultural literacy learning. She did not exclude holidays associated with usual "American" traditions, but added holidays from around the world. There was learning about Christmas, Hannukah, and the Chinese New Year. Instead of creating activities based exclusively on St. Patrick's

Day, the children studied Ireland and spring customs around the world. Mrs. Starr also realized that the ESL teacher, Mrs. Brown, studied customs from around the world in her program, so she decided to ask her to share knowledge with the kindergarten class.

In the past, Mrs. Starr had only briefly communicated with Mrs. Brown. The exchanges occasionally occurred when Mrs. Brown appeared at the classroom door twice a week to pull students for half-hour English studies. The children who were in the ESL program often resisted leaving a reading lesson or learning center activity. They would frown, cry, or ask why they had to leave. When the steering committee formed, Mrs. Starr met with Mrs. Brown and began talking about an inclusive ESL program in the kindergarten. At first Mrs. Brown hesitated. Mrs. Starr reported:

> Mrs. Brown believed that her children had special needs. They needed time to talk in small quiet groups. Mrs. Brown wondered what she would do in my class. I asked her to share her knowledge with the class; I would help her plan. I assured her that this was something we would try and wouldn't be written in stone.

When Mrs. Brown agreed, Mrs. Starr worked around Mrs. Brown's schedule, which included travel among three schools. They quickly planned during fifteen-minute and half-hour blocks of time at lunch and after school and created both a coordinated pull-out and a push-in lesson each week. Their efforts produced positive results:

> Mrs. Brown and I coordinated our schedules to fit a push-in class once a week. We read stories from other cultures and prepared multicultural activities. Our ESL students and other students shared their cultures and were visibly excited about exploring peoples and places around the world.

Mrs. Starr and the ESL teacher believed the literacy learning program needed a greater emphasis on multicultural literature. They read aloud books recommended by the school librarian, classroom teachers, and those studied in a children's literature graduate course. Also, with the steering committee, Mrs. Starr and Mrs. Brown began to search and study catalogs and book lists of multicultural literature. Mrs. Starr noted with satisfaction:

> This year I learned to read books carefully to find out the cultural messages and ideas they were portraying. Through these messages and ideas, lessons about cultural diversity emerged. Books were read for enjoyment, as specific reading lessons with follow-up activities, and as part of the push-in ESL lesson for the whole class.

Mrs. Starr was pleased with her classroom changes related to holidays and celebrations, literature and her work with Mrs. Brown's ESL program. She could see change and the results seemed good for the children. Additionally, she talked about personal change related to her classroom experiences:

> The successes with my class made me realize how little I knew before I began this project. I had never actually worked or socialized with people different from my own background. I was not given any training to help understand people who are different from me. I thought that we should tolerate and not talk about differences. I thought students would feel better and learn better if we ignored differences.

Mrs. Starr now saw her classroom as a more interesting learning place and was aware that what she had learned benefited all of the children.

Changes in Other Classrooms

Mrs. Starr hoped the steering committee members would begin to use the ideas she was implementing in her classroom, but not all members seemed as interested in making change in their classrooms. Mrs. Starr explained:

> All the teachers on the committee love a good book for children, so the multicultural literature study created a lot of enthusiasm, but not all of the teachers read the books aloud or created activities related to other cultures and their holidays. Their reactions seemed to show cultural conflict.

One teacher believed the students would be confused about "American" traditions if too many other cultures were introduced. Another teacher did not have language-minority children in her classroom, so did not see that it made sense to teach about other cultures unless they were present. Both teachers were concerned about preserving what they believed to be "American" traditions.

Kites, paper cranes, songs, dances, food, holidays and languages of other cultures were part of Mrs. Starr's classroom and a first grade teacher's classroom. However, the ESL teacher worked only in Mrs. Starr's classroom. The first grade teacher did not believe that her language-minority student would receive enough help with the English language if he was not pulled from the classroom for special help. Because his Cambodian home culture was so different from the school culture, she believed that he had to learn to fit into the school culture.

Mrs. Starr was surprised and disappointed with her colleagues' reactions. However, she believed it was important to provide a model for change, so she remained positive and reported her own classroom results at steering committee meetings. She reflected:

> I tried not to show my disappointment. I tried to understand their difficulties and offer possible suggestions. I would also explain what I was doing and how I was doing it, but the "fit in" perspective or assimilationist perspective was a very strong influence. Even though they talked about appreciating diversity, they still seemed to want everyone to be the same.

Reflections on Changes Between Home and School

One of the steering committee's major objectives was to improve communication with language-minority parents. The members of the committee agreed that it might be possible to get the parents involved in culturally diverse activities within the classroom. They discussed Faltis' (1993) four-levels approach for communicating with multilingual parents. Level I describes the early stages of teacher-parent informal contacts in the home and school. Level II explains how to proceed to small informational meetings. Level III gives examples of ways to encourage parent participation and sharing in the classroom. Level IV tells about parent empowerment when they are included in curricular decisions. Mrs. Starr immediately began to strengthen her communication with parents using the approach:

> I reached out to the parents. I visited their homes and asked them to teach me about their home country, language, travels and customs. They began to trust me and share. Eventually they shared in my classroom.

Through a parent form letter created and developed by the steering committee, all parents were encouraged to become involved in classrooms by sharing hobbies, interests, and cultures. Twenty-five of a possible forty families gave presentations in Mrs. Starr's classroom. Parents taught a wide variety of classroom activities, such as scientific experiments with dry ice, sign language, wood carving, and Ukranian Easter egg decoration. Of the seven language-minority families, five made presentations in the classroom and two gave Mrs. Starr the information and artifacts to share. She reflected:

> The Vietnamese, Native American, Hispanic, Italian, Ukranian, Jewish and Korean cultures were presented. The classroom globe became a favorite place to gather in the mornings as students found countries related to the cultures they studied.

Mrs. Starr sent home an information sheet at the end of the school year. It was also created by the steering committee for the purpose of gathering parent reactions to multicultural education. Parents were asked to sit with their children and record their comments on the list of the year's activities. In Mrs. Starr's kindergarten, all of the language-minority parents and all but five of the other parents responded. Representative parent comments demonstrate the progress made in her class:

"I think that it is very important to teach children at an early age that differences in people does not mean wrong."

"I'm so happy you teach my child and other kids about my country."

"My child like talk our language in your class. He feel important."

"I was amazed to see how much my child remembered about each cultural project."

"We found this year to be very educational for our child. It helped him learn that just because somebody has a different color skin or talks different doesn't mean any better or worse than he is."

"I think learning about different countries and their people and cultures is wonderful for setting the groundwork in making our children understand that we are different but yet we are all the same."

Only one parent expressed concerns, "I wouldn't light those Jewish candles (Menorah) at Christmas; we're not Jewish. They were thrown out."

Mrs. Starr was pleased with most parent reactions. She expressed her feelings openly:

> Parent involvement during this school year was tremendous in my classroom. Parents were visible on almost a daily basis. They were

comfortable enough to make presentations and be involved in class activities. The children enjoyed the parent lessons.

At the end of the school year, Mrs. Starr reported that she had not only strengthened her communication with language-minority parents, but with all of her children's parents.

Changes Between Home and School in Other Classes

Mrs. Starr's successes with parents were not experienced by other members of the committee. Even though the steering committee actually created the home and school communication forms and sent them home, the teachers did not actively follow up with home visits, phone calls, or letters. One teacher explained that her language-minority parents acted embarrassed when she asked them to share their culture: "They have not been asked to do this in the past. They feel uncomfortable with it."

Another teacher stated that the parent of a child recommended for ESL would not allow the child to get help in the program. "I could not make the parent understand." Raji's mother was now assisting in that classroom and would not consent to Raji's leaving. The ESL teacher was not coordinating lessons with the classroom teacher, so Raji's parents, based on the previous year's experiences, did not believe it would be helpful for him to miss the work in the classroom. The classroom teacher remarked,

> Time is not available in the school day for making contact with the ESL teacher or language-minority parents, since schedules and English language difficulties make arrangements difficult.

Mrs. Starr realized that the time factor was real and that it took a lot of extra time to reach out to her parents. She explained the reactions of her colleagues on the steering committee:

> They told me that my kindergarten parents don't know what has happened in the past so they willingly filled out forms, accepted the multicultural activities and the inclusive ESL program without question. I agreed that they were probably correct. Kindergarten might be the place to start with new school ideas.

Mrs. Starr was disappointed in steering committee reactions to home and school communications, but she seemed to understand why. She stated:

> I believe that some teachers on the steering committee feel uncomfortable with other cultures, because they feel unsure of how to communicate. They have strong feelings about "American traditions" and are afraid to take risks. They needed a demonstration and I took the risks. Their observations of my successes may encourage them in the future.

Mrs. Starr recognized the teachers' perceptions, but maintained the determination to continue with her own efforts. She did not give up the hope for change because of the successes in her own classroom. But she also learned that through the quest for change, barriers for change may emerge.

Reflections on Conflict: Responses To Change

Mrs. Starr reflected upon what she believed to be the cultural conflicts which she saw emerging as she attempted to make change in the school. Conflicts occurred among the kindergarten staff, the multicultural education steering committee, and the administration. "To many teachers and administrators, 'change' is not a nice word."

Kindergarten staff. The kindergarten program created by the team of three kindergarten teachers and two teaching assistants had never emphasized the teaching of cultural diversity. Multicultural literacy learning activities were also not in their personal or professional experiences. When the steering committee began meeting, Mrs. Starr reported committee objectives to the kindergarten staff:

> I will be teaching new ideas related to multicultural education in my class this year. I will be sharing the ideas with you, but I certainly don't expect you to do them unless you wish to try. They should not interfere with our present program.

As the year progressed, Mrs. Starr began to feel tensions during team meetings. Because of the numerous parent presentations in her classroom, she was not participating in videos and other whole group kindergarten activities. One team member commented when Mrs. Starr missed a video, "Oh, I forgot! You're into that multicultural stuff!" Also, when Mrs. Starr stated that she was not going to participate in the annual St. Patrick's Day celebration, but attempt an "Around the World Spring Party," the comment was, "I think you're forgetting about America."

Mrs. Starr was hurt by the comments, but responded

positively by attempting to involve her team in a few of the activities. She purchased multicultural crayons for each kindergarten child on the team and distributed them to the teachers. She shared some of the activities which could be accomplished and displayed her children's work related to similarities and differences in skin color and facial characteristics. The staff complimented her on the lessons, but at the end of the year when she collected the crayons, none had been used in their classrooms. Mrs. Starr rationalized, "Maybe they just aren't ready to try these ideas."

Steering committee. Mrs. Starr saw cultural conflict appear within the steering committee. One teacher was uncomfortable with the idea of working with the ESL teacher in the classroom since she believed the school schedule was too full to allow time for learning about other languages and cultures. Also, committee members who created and developed cultural information packets and parent surveys did not aggressively follow with phone calls and letters. They stated, "I sent them home, but they haven't been returned,"or "The parents don't understand them," or "They haven't done anything like this in the past." Mrs.Starr countered:

> We have to make the extra effort when working with our language-minority parents. They don't feel comfortable yet. Mine have responded, because I visited their homes, called often and/or sent notes. We have to show them we care before they will trust us.

Mrs. Starr was discouraged with the committee's reactions, but she reasoned, "The committee is unsure about investing time and energy into home and school communication since I think they're unsure of their own understandings of multicultural literacy learning."

Administration. Administrators were another group that seemed conflicted about change. At first the assistant superintendent and principal appeared interested. However, after one month into the school year, Mrs. Starr received a note from her principal stating, "Dr. Stack is concerned about the multicultural education project. He does not want it to become a big issue in the school district, so your work should be confined to our school."

Mrs. Starr expressed surprise. "I couldn't believe it! I felt deflated. How could he say that? I almost feel like I am doing something wrong."

Furthermore, two requests made to the administration during the year received no responses. First, Mrs. Starr asked for translators at parent conferences since she heard that they were available at a local volunteer organization. Second, the ESL teacher made a written and oral request for more time to work with teachers for the planning of inclusive ESL classroom programs.

Finally, the steering committee wrote a proposal for summer curriculum work. In the past, committee proposals were always accepted by the school district administrators' council which reviews summer proposals, but this year was different. Mrs. Starr described the rationale for the proposal:

> We wanted to create a list of multicultural literature and activities to be used within our school. It would be a resource for the teachers which would encourage an awareness of other cultures. The principal informed us that our proposal was not accepted, but she told us that she didn't know why.

Mrs. Starr expressed concerns about the administration's reactions since other schools in the district were beginning to see an influx of language-minority students. There seemed to be an apparent need to address diversity. She conjectured:

> Maybe the administration doesn't understand the growing need? Maybe they choose to ignore diversity, since they fear the cost in time and money?

Mrs. Starr, surprised by administration responses, could only guess why they were not demonstrating an interest in a project which she perceived as important for children.

Summary of Changes

Mrs. Starr was somewhat disappointed in the schoolwide results of the project, but her own classroom successes produced the impetus to continue the effort. The conflicts that emerged gave her a better understanding of the obstacles which lay ahead. She reflected:

> I realize that my project deals mainly with the first stages of multicultural education; we concentrated on literature and holidays as described by James Banks (1997) and Rasinski & Padak (1990). We have

much more to do, but the school staff seems resistant. They want children from other cultures, to fit into the classroom, forget about their home cultures and learn about this country only.

The obstacles perceived after her year-long study (Squires, 1993) are similar to those documented in the research on resistance to change in regard to multicultural agendas. Researchers confirm Mrs. Starr's discoveries that the assimilationist perspective and racist attitudes often prevail in school settings (Goodlad & Oakes, 1988; Cummins, 1989; Treuba, et al., 1990; Lee, 1993). Faculty and staff encourage minority students to fit into what they believe is the "American" culture at the expense of the children's home language and culture. Consequently, the literacy development necessary for successful academic and social experiences in the American school is harmed (Ogbu, 1978; Cummins, 1989; Reyhner & Garcia, 1989; Goldenberg, 1990; Trueba, et al., 1990; Snow, 1992). Mrs. Starr could see that it is difficult to change beliefs which have been nationally accepted for so many years.

Mrs. Starr also understood that there were several important factors to consider in the process for change. First, her colleagues were reluctant to take ownership of the project; it was basically her idea. The steering committee and the kindergarten staff either ignored the project or became minimally involved. She realized that she was the only one who actually saw an urgent need for change. She also realized that the discussion of ideas for change and a plan for change do not necessarily translate into classroom practice.

Similarly, researchers who study change in schools suggest that teachers must perceive a need for change in their own classrooms and make specific plans related to their students in order for change to occur (Vacca, 1989; Courtland, 1992). Additionally, there are studies which demonstrate that in the school hierarchy, kindergarten teachers are given lower status (Hargreaves, 1988; Goodson, 1992; Hargreaves & Fullan, 1992); thus they may not be perceived as leaders in the change process. Finally, recent research on the ability of teachers to connect teaching and leadership skills (Wasley, 1991; Leogrande, 1995) report that it is often difficult for teachers to combine both teaching and leadership roles.

Mrs. Starr, as the teacher leader of the project, found that she could make change in her own classroom but had difficulties influencing change in other classrooms. Therefore, when her master's degree project (Squires, 1993) was officially completed, she asked the steering committee to select a new leader. Being a teacher member rather than a teacher leader, she hoped that the committee would take charge and see it as a schoolwide project.

Second, Mrs. Starr recognized that the change process was linked to time. Researchers propose that the time factor is crucial for change (Feeley & Strickland, 1989; Vacca, 1994). Related to time is the fact that classroom isolation prevents team-based talk (Little, 1993; McLaughlin, 1993). She and her colleagues had little time to share and reflect daily upon new ideas implemented in their classrooms and claimed that excessive amounts of time were needed to reach out to diverse groups of parents. Mrs. Starr agreed, but she believed that if she provided a successful model for change in her own classroom, colleagues might eventually minimize the time factor when they heard about the benefits to children and their families. Also, she hoped administrators would observe her work and become aware of the need for more time to communicate and plan among the parents and teachers. Administrators have numerous demands on their time, but they often are in positions which allow the restructuring of time for the implementation of change.

Third, Mrs. Starr learned that the issues related to multicultural literacy learning were much more complex than she had originally thought. The first year of change was punctuated with conflict. She believed the conflict occurred when colleagues did not appear to see a need for understanding the increasingly diverse populations in classrooms. Mrs. Starr contended that the steering committee's reluctance to change may have been associated with the school culture as well as the the school district's hesitancy about promoting multicultural education. She also concluded that many of her colleagues embraced the assimilationist perspective (Cummins, 1989; Porter, 1990), which expects minorities to fit into the dominant "American" culture as quickly as possible for economic success. She also was confronted with her colleagues' fears of losing the "American" culture with the promotion of world cultures. She even considered that possible racist attitudes may have influenced the conflicts (Derman-Sparks, 1992; Lee 1991; Oakes & Quartz, 1995).

Since research reveals that few educators are aware of the need for understanding and appreciating cultural diversity in the classroom (Penfield, 1987; Faltis, 1989; 1993), faculty and staff must thoroughly examine new information which demonstrates the need for change before significant change can take place

(Vacca 1992; 1994; DeCorse, 1996). At the end of the school year, members of the steering committee did acknowledge that a better understanding of multicultural literacy learning was important to them. Therefore, they began to talk about enrolling in multicultural education courses offered at nearby colleges. Additionally, they listed possible guest presentations and workshops from students, parents, teachers, and researchers involved in multicultural education. The committee scheduled meetings for next year with additional members added in the fall; the principal was encouraged to attend. Mrs. Starr perceived these steps as opportunities for gaining knowledge and making progress for the change process to continue.

Finally, despite of the conflicts experienced during the year, Mrs. Starr remained hopeful. She saw the progress in her own classroom and the steering committee's attempts to learn. She believed her own teammates would begin to try some of the successes observed in her classroom, and, finally, she concluded that the administration would eventually come to terms with cultural diversity. She analyzed the year:

> I think many educators are unfamiliar with multicultural literacy learning, but I hope this year will begin the changes in classroom practices, home-school communication, and administration responses. If I continue my work in my classroom and continue membership in the steering committee, I believe my colleagues will begin to understand the need for change. Then, with time, trust, and knowledge, we can make a difference.

In summary, change in an imperfect world is difficult. As Hargreaves (in press) states: "So the paradox of educational change needing to be both fast and slow, narrow and broad, need not be a paradox of despair. It can be a paradox of hope... through small but significant initiatives..."(p.253). Similarly, Mrs. Starr's reflections upon the year are positive:

> It can be difficult to work for change, but I see the first year as the beginning. I will continue my efforts for change along with other faculty and staff. I believe multicultural literacy learning encourages an appreciation of diversity. It enriches the classroom, promotes social justice, and in the long run, helps to reduce school drop-out...and that's good for everyone.

Reference List

Adams, M. J. (1991). *Beginning to read: Thinking and learning about print.* Cambridge MA: The MIT Press.

Atkin, J. M. (1991). *Teaching as research.* Paper presented at the annual meeting of the American Educational Research Association, Chicago.

Au, K. (1993). *Literacy instruction in multicultural settings.* New York: Harcourt, Brace Jovanovich.

Au, K., & Mason. J. (1981). Social organizational factors in learning to read: The balance of rights hypothesis. *Reading Research Quarterly, 17*(1), 115-152.

Ball, E. W., & Blachman, B. A. (1991). Does phoneme awareness training in kindergarten make a difference in early word recognition and developmental spelling? *Reading Research Quarterly, 26*(1), 49-66.

Ballenger, C. (1992). Because you like us: The language of control. *Harvard Educational Review, 62*(2), 199-208.

Banks, J.A. (1997). *Teaching strategies for ethnic studies* (6th ed.). Boston: Allyn & Bacon.

Barone, D. (1996). Whose language? Learning from bilingual learners in a developmental first grade classroom. In D. J. Leu, C. K. Kinzer & K.A. Hinchman (Eds.), *Literacies for the 21st Century: Research and Practice.* Forty-fifth yearbook of the National Reading Conference. Chicago, IL: National Reading Conference.

Barrera, R. B. (1992). The cultural gap in literature-based literacy instruction. *Education and Urban Society.* 24(2), 227-243.

Battle, J. (1993). Mexican-American bilingual kindergarteners' collaborations in meaning making. In D.J. Leu & C.K. Kinzer (Eds.), *Examining central issues in literacy research, theory and practice.* Forty-second yearbook of the National Reading Conference. Chicago, IL: National Reading Conference.

Berends, M. (1992). *A description of restructuring in nationally nominated schools.* Paper presented at the annual meeting of the American Educational Research Association, San Francisco.

Blanchard, E. L. (1983). The growth and development of American Indian and Alaskan Native children. In G. J. Powell (Ed.), *The psychosocial development of minority group children.*

Bloome, D. (1986). Building literacy and the classroom community. *Theory into Practice, 15*(2), 71-76. New York: Brunner/Mazel Publishers.

Bloome, D., & Green, J. (1982). The social contexts of reading: A multi-disciplinary perspective. In B. A. Hutson (Ed.), *Advances in reading/language research* (Vol. 1, pp. 309-338). Greenwich, CT: JAI Press.

Blumer, H. (1969). *Symbolic interactionism: Perspective and method.* Englewood Cliffs, NJ: Prentice-Hall.

Bogdan, R. C. (1972). *Participant observation in organizational settings.* Syracuse, NY: Syracuse University Press.

Bogdan, R. C., & Biklen, S. K. (1994). *Qualitative research for education: An introduction to theory and methods.* Boston, MA: Allyn and Bacon.

Bond, G. L., & Dykstra, R. (1967). The cooperative research program in first grade reading instruction. *Reading Research Quarterly, 2*(5), 142-152.

Britton, J. Shafer, R. E., & Watson, K. (Eds.). (1990). *Teaching and learning English Worldwide.* IFTE: Multilingual Matters.

Cardenas, J. A. (1977). Response I. In N. A. Epstein (Ed.), *Language, ethnicity and the schools: Policy alternatives for bilingual-bicultural education.* Washington, D.C.: Institute for Educational Leadership, George Washington University.

Chall, J. (1967). *Learning to read: The great debate.* New York: McGraw-Hill.

Chomsky, C. (1972). Stages in language development and reading exposure. *Harvard Educational Review, 42*,1-33.

Clay, M. M. (1971). The Polynesian language skills of Maori and Samoan school entrants. *International Journal of Psychology,* pp. 135-145.

Clay, M. M. (1976). Early childhood and cultural diversity in New Zealand. *The Reading Teacher, 29*(4), 333-342.

Courtland, M. C. (1992). Teacher change in the implementation of new approaches to literacy instruction. In J. Vacca (Ed.). *Bringing about change in schools* (pp. 30-36). Newark, DE: International Reading Association.

Crowell, D.C., Kawakami, A.J., & Wong, J.L. (1986). Emerging literacy: Reading-writing experiences in a kindergarten classroom. *Reading Teacher, 40*(2), 144-149.

Cuban, L. (1989). The 'at-risk' label and the problem of urban school reform. *Phi Delta Kappan, 70*(10), 780-801.

Cummins, J. (1980). The cross-lingual dimensions of language proficiency: Implications for immigrant language learning and bilingual education. *TESOL Quarterly, 14,* 175-187.

Cummins, J. (1986). Empowering minority students: A framework for intervention. *Harvard Educational Review, 56*(1), 18-36.

Cummins, J. (1989). *Empowering minority students.* Sacramento:

California Association for Bilingual Education Publications.

Cummins, J. (1996). Forward. In S. Nieto, *Affirming diversity: The sociopolitical context of multicultural education (2nd ed.).* (pp. xv-xvii). New York: Longman.

DeCorse, C. B. (1996). Teachers and the integrated curriculum: An intergenerational view. *Action in Teacher Education, 18*(1), 85-92.

Delgado-Gaitian, C. (1989). *Literacy for empowerment.* Basingstoke, England: The Falmer Press.

Derman-Sparks, L. (1992). *Anti-bias curriculum: Tools for empowering young children.* Sacramento: California State Department of Education.

Diaz, R. (1983). Thought and two languages: The impact of bilingualism on cognitive development. *Review of Research in Education, 10,* 23-54.

Divoky, D. (1988). The model minority goes to school. *Phi Delta Kappan, 70*(3), 219-222.

Duncan, J, (1996). Using facilitated communication in classrooms. *The Facilitated Communication Digest, 2*(2), 15 -17.

Dresser, N. (1994). *I felt like I was from another planet.* New York: Addison-Wesley Publishing Company.

Dyson, A. H. (1989). *Multiple worlds of child writers: Friends learning to write.* New York: Teachers College Press.

Dyson, A. H. (1993). *Whistle for Willie,* lost puppies, and cartoon dogs: The sociocultural dimensions of young children's composing. *Journal of Reading Behavior, 24*(4), 433-462.

Early, M. (1990). Enabling first and second language learners in the classroom. *Language Arts, 67,* 567-575.

Edelsky, C. (1986). *Writing in a bilingual program: Habia una vez.* Norwood, NJ: Ablex Publishing Corporation.

Edwards, D., & Mercer, N. (1989). Reconstructing context: The conventionalization of classroom knowledge. *Discourse Processes, 12,* 91-104.

Edwards, P. A. (1996). Creating sharing time conversations: Parents and teachers work together. *Language Arts, 73,* 344 - 349.

Ehri, L. C. (1976). Word learning in beginning readers and prereaders: Effects of form class and defining contexts. *Journal of Educational Psychology, 67,* 204-212.

Elbaz, F. (1991). Research on teacher's knowledge. *Journal of Curriculum Studies, 23*(1), 5-16.

Faltis, C. (1989). Preparing bilingual teachers for cultural diversity. *New York Association of Bilingual Education,*

5(2), 17-26.

Faltis, C. J. (1993). *Joinfostering: Adapting teaching strategies for the multilingual classroom.* New York: Maxwell Macmillan International.

Farrell, E. J. (1991). Instructional models for English language arts, K-12. In J. Flood, J. M. Jenson, D. Lapp, and J. R. Squire (Eds.), *Handbook of research on teaching the English language arts* (pp. 63-84). New York: Macmillan.

Feeley, J. T. (1983). Help for the reading teacher: Dealing with the limited English proficiency (LEP) child in the elementary classroom. *The Reading Teacher, 36*(4), 650-655.

Feeley, J. T., & Strickland, D. S. (1989). Time. In S. B. Wepner, J. T. Feeley & D. S. Strickland (Eds.). *The administration and supervision of reading programs.* New York: Teachers College Press.

Fein, G. (1975). A transformational analysis of pretending. *Developmental Psychology, 11,* 291-296.

Figueroa,R.A. (1989). Psychological testing of linguistic minority students: Knowledge gaps and regulations. *Exceptional Children, 56*(2), 145-152.

Fishman, J. (1989). *Language and ethnicity in minority sociolinguistic perspective.* New York: Multilingual Matters.

Franks, M. E. (November 1988). *Using the gap reduction model to evaluate a successful bilingual/ESL program.* Paper presented at the 17Th annual meeting of the Mid-south Educational Research Association. Louisville, KY.

Fullan, M., & Hargreaves, A. (1991). *What's worth fighting for in your school?* Toronto: Ontario Public School Teacher's Federation.

Fullan, M. (1993). *Change forces: Probing the depths of educational reform.* London: Falmer Press.

Garcia, E. (1986). Bilingual development and the education of bilingual children during early childhood. In B. Spodek, (Ed.). *Today's kindergarten: Exploring the knowledge base, expanding the curriculum.* New York and London: Teachers College Press.

Garcia, E. (1994). *Understanding and meeting the challenge of student cultural diversity.* Boston: Houghton Mifflin Company.

Gardner, H. (1991). *The unschooled mind: How children think and how schools should teach.* New York: Basic Books.

Geertz, C. (1973). Thick description: Toward an interpretive theory of culture. In *The interpretation of cultures.* New York: Basic Books.

Glaser, B. G., & Strauss, A. L. (1967). *The discovery of grounded*

143

theory: strategies for qualitative research. New York: Aldine DeGruyter.

Goldenberg, C. N. (1987). Low-income Hispanic parents' contributions to their first-grade children's word-recognition skills. *Anthropology and Education Quarterly, 18,* 149-179.

Good, T., & Brophy, J. (1991). *Looking into classrooms.* New York: HarperCollins.

Goodlad, J. (1991). Why we need a complete redesign of teacher education. *Educational Leadership, 49* (3), 4-10.

Goodlad, J., & Oakes, J. (1988). We must offer equal access to knowledge. *Educational Leadership, 45*(5), 16-22.

Goodmann, K. (1986). *What's whole in whole language?* Portsmouth, NH: Heinemann.

Goodman, K., & Goodman, Y. (1990). Vygotsky and a whole language perspective. In L. C. Moll (Ed.), *Vygotsky and education (pp. 223-250).* Cambridge, England: Cambridge University Press.

Goodson, I. F. (1992). Sponsoring the teacher's voice. In A. Hargreaves, and M. Fullan (Eds.), *Understanding teacher development.* New York: Teacher's College Press.

Gougis, R. A. (1986). The effects of prejudice and stress on the academic achievement of Black Americans. In U. Neisser (Ed.), *The school achievement of minority children: New perspectives.* Hillsdale, NJ: Erlbaum.

Green, J., Kantor R., & Rogers, T. (1990). Exploring the complexity of lnaguage and learning in the classroom. In B. Jones, & L. Idol (Eds.), *Educational values and cognitive instruction: Implications for reform, Vol.3 (pp. 333-364).* Hillsdale, NJ: Erlbaum.

Gump, P. (1989). Ecological psychology and issues of play. In M. Bloch & A. D. Pelligrini (Eds.), *The ecological context of children's play* (pp. 35-56). Norwood, NJ: Ablex.

Gumperz , J. (1986). Interactional sociolinguistics in the study of schooling. In J. Cook-Gumperz (Ed.), *The social contruction of literacy* (pp.45-68). Cambridge, England: Cambridge University Press.

Hakuta, K. (1986). *Mirror of language: The debate on bilingualism.* NY: Basic Books.

Hargreaves, A. (1988). Teaching quality: A sociological analysis. *Journal of Curriculum Studies, 20*(3), 211-231.

Hargreaves, A. & Fullan, M. (Eds.). (1992). *Understanding teacher development.* New York: Teachers College Press.

Hargreaves, A. (1996). Revisiting voice. *Educational Researcher,*

25(1), 12-19.

Hargreaves, A. (in press). Getting there. In A. Hargreaves, L. Earl, & J. Ryan, *Schooling for change: Educating young adolescents for tomorrow's world* (pp. 227-253). New York: Falmer Press.

Hatton, E. (1989). Levi-Strauss's Bricolage and theorizing teachers' work. *Anthropology and Education Quarterly, 20(2),* 74-96.

Heath, S. B. (1983). *Ways with words: Language, life and work in communities and classrooms.* Cambridge: Cambridge University Press.

Herber, H.L., & Herber, J. N. (1993). *Teaching in content areas with reading writing and reasoning.* Boston: Allyn and Bacon.

Hoffman, E. (1989). *Lost in translation: A life in a new language.* New York: Penguin Books.

Holdaway, D. (1979). *The foundations of literacy.* Sydney, Australia: Ashton Scholastic.

Igoa, C. (1995). *The inner world of the immigrant child.* New York: St. Martin's Press.

Jackson, G., & Cosca, C. (1974). The inequality of educational opportunity in the Southwest: An observational study of ethnically mixed classrooms. *American Educational Journal,* 11, 219-229.

Jacob, E., & Sanday, P. R. (1976). Dropping out: A strategy for coping with cultural pluralism. In P.R. Sanday (Ed.), *Anthropology and the public interest: Fieldwork and theory* (pp. 95-110). New York: Academic Press.

Kalantzis, M., Cope, B., Noble, G., & Poynting, S. (Eds.). (1990). *Cultures of schooling: Pedagogies for cultural difference and social access.* Wollongong University Australia: Palmer Press.

Kaminsky, S. (1976). Bilingualism and learning to read. In A. Simpes (Ed.), *The Bilingual Child.* New York: Academic Press.

Kantor, R., Miller, S., & Fernie, D. (1992). Diverse paths to literacy in a preschool classroom: A sociocultural perspective. *Reading Research Quarterly, 27(3),* 185-201.

Keats, E. J. (1962). A snowy day. New York, NY: Puffin Books.

Kidder, T. (1989). *Among schoolchildren.* New York: Avon Books.

Kiefer, B. Z., & DeStefano, J. S. (1985). Cultures together in the classroom: "What you sayin?" In A. M. Jagger & M. Smith-Burke (Eds.), *On observing the language learner.* Newark, DE: International Reading Association and Urbana IL: NCTE.

Kincheloe, J. L., & Steinberg, S. R. (1993). A tentative description of post-formal thinking: The critical confrontation with cognitive theory. *Harvard Educational Review, 63*(3), 296-320.

Kleifgen, J. (1990). Prekindergarten children's second discourse learning. *Discourse Processes, 13*, 225-242.

Kochman, T. (1983). The boundary between play and nonplay in Black verbal dueling. *Language in Society, 12*, 239-337.

Lee, E. (1993). An interview with educator Enid Lee: Taking multicultural, antiracist education seriously, *Rethinking Schools*, 3, 6 -10.

Leogrande, C. (1995). *Teaching and leadership: Bridging two worlds.* Unpublished doctoral dissertation, Syracuse University, Syracuse, NY.

Leu, D. & Kinzer, C. (1986). *Effective reading instruction in the elementary grades*. Columbus, Ohio: Merrill Publishing Company.

Levine, S. (1987). Using a multicultural language arts program involving school, home, and community to increase students' reading achievement and the elementary school faculty's knowledge of their students' diverse cultures. *Ed. D. Practicum,* Nova University. ED286168.

Lincoln, Y., & Guba, E. (1985). *Naturalistic inquiry.* Beverly Hills CA: Sage.

Little, J. W. (1993). Teachers' professional development in a climate of educational reform. *Educational Evaluation and Policy Analysis,* 15(2), 129-152.

Long, M. H. (1980). Inside the 'black box': Methodological issues on classroom research on language learning. *Language Learning,* 30, 1-42.

Martin, J.H. (1984). *IBM writing to read.* Coral Springs, Florida: IBM.

McCaleb, S. P. (1994). *Building communities of learners.* New York: St. Martin's Press.

McKay, S. (1988). Weighing educational alternatives. In McKay, S., and Wong, S. (Eds.), *Language diversity: Problem or resource?* (pp. 338-361). New York: Newbury House.

Milner, D. (1983). *Children and race: Ten years on.* London: Ward Lock Educational.

Miramontes, O.(December 1992). *Language and learning: Exploring schooling issues that impact linguistically diverse students.* Keynote address at the 42nd Annual National Reading conference, San Antonio, Texas.

Moll, L. C. (Ed.). (1990). *Vygotsky and education.* Cambridge, England: Cambridge University Press.

Moll, L. C. (1992). Bilingual classroom studies and community analysis: Some recent trends. *Educational Researcher, 21*(2), 20-24.

Moll, L. C., & Diaz, S. (1987). Change as a goal of educational research. *Anthropology and Education Quarterly, 18,* 300 -311.

Moll, L. C., & Greenberg, J. (1990). Creating zones of possibilities: Combining social contexts for instruction. In. L. C. Moll (Ed.),*Vygotsky and Education* (pp.319-348). Cambridge, England: Cambridge University Press.

Neuman, S., & Roskos, K. (1992). Literacy objects as cultural tools: Effects on children's literacy behaviors in play. *Reading Research Quarterly 27*(3), 203-226.

Nickse, R. S., Speicher, A. M., & Buchek, P. (1988). An intergenerational adult literacy project: A family intervention/prevention model. *Journal of Reading,31,* 634-642.

Nieto, S. (1996). *Affirming diversity: The sociopolitical context of multicultural education.* New York: Longman.

Oakes, J., & Quartz, K. H. (Eds.). (1995). *Creating new educational communities.* Ninety-fourth yearbook for the National Society for the Study of Education, part I. Chicago, IL: National Society for the Study of Education

Ogbu, J. (1978). *Minority education and caste.* New York: Harcourt Brace, Jovonovich.

Ogbu, J.U. (1983). Minority status and schooling in plural societies. *Comparative Educational Review, 27*(2), 168-190.

Ogbu, J.U. (1987). Variability in minority performance: A problem in search of explanation. *Anthropology and Education Quarterly, 18*(4), 312-334.

Olson, L. (1990). misreading said to hamper Hispanics' role in school. *Education Week, 9*(32), 4.

Ortiz, F. I. (1988). Hispanic-American children's experiences in classrooms: A comparison between Hispanic and non-Hispanic students. In L. Weis (Ed.), *Class, race and gender in American education.* Albany: State University of New York Press.

Palinscar, A. M. (1989). Less charted waters. *Educational Researcher, 18*(4), 5-7.

Pattnaik, J. (1996). *Defining culture: Preservice teachers perceptions of an Asian instructor.* Symposium paper, 1996 National Reading Conference 46th Annual Meeting, Charleston, SC, December 4-7.

Paulston, C. B. (1980). *Bilingual education: Theories and issues.* Rowley, MA: Newbury House.

Pearson, P. D., Johnson, D. D., Clymer, T., Indisano, R., Venezky, R., Bauman, J., Hiebert, E., & Toth, M. (1991). *World of reading*. New York: Silver Burdett and Ginn.

Penfield, J. (1987). ESL: The regular classroom teacher's perspective. *TESOL Quarterly, 21*(1), 21-39.

Percell, C. H. (1989). Social class and educational equality. In J. Banks and C. A. McGee Banks, *Multicultural education: Issues and perspectives*. Boston: Allyn & Bacon.

Peter, J. (1994). Examining the participation of young, linguistically diverse children at a writing center. In C. Kinzer & D. Leu, *Multidimensional aspects of literacy, research, theory and practice*. Chicago, IL: National Reading Conference.

Phillips, S. (1982). *The invisible culture: Communication in classroom and community on the Warm Springs Indian Reservation*. New York: Longman.

Piestrup, A. M. (1973). *Black dialect interference and accomodations for reading instruction in first grade*. (Language and Behavior Research Lab, Monograph No. 4). University of California at Berkeley.

Place, K., & Becker, J. (1991). The influence of pragmatic competence on the likeability of grade school children. *Discourse Processes, 14*, 227-241.

Porter, R. (1990). *Forked Tongue: The politics of bilingual education*. New York: Basic Books.

Powell, G. J. (1983). Coping with adversity: The psychosocial development of Afro-American Children. In G. J. Powell, *The psychosocial development of minority group children*. New York: Brunner/Mazel Publishers.

Quintero, E., & Huerta-Macias, A. (1990). All in the family: bilingualism and biliteracy. *The ReadingTeacher, 44*(4), 306-312.

Rasinski, T. V., & Padak, N. D. (1990). Multicultural learning through children's literature. *Language arts, 67,* 576-580.

Resnick, L. (1990). Literacy in school and out. *Daedelus, 19*(2), 169-185.

Reyhner, J., & Garcia, R. L. (1989). Helping minorities read better: Problems and promises. *Reading research and instruction, 28*(3), 84-91.

Rigg, P., & Allen, V.G. (Eds.). (1989). *When they don't all speak English: Integrating the ESL student in the regular classroom*. Urbana, IL: NCTE.

Rist, R.. (1973). *The urban school: A factory for failure*. Cambridge, MA: MIT Press.

148

Rist, R..(1978). *The invisible children*. Cambridge, MA: Harvard University Press.

Rodriguez, R. (1982). *Hunger of memory: The education of Richard Rodriguez*. New York: Bantam Books.

Rogoff, B. (1986). Adult assistance of children's learning. In T. E. Raphael (Ed.), *Contexts of school based literacy* (pp. 27-40).

Rotberg, I. A. (1982). Some legal and research considerations in establishing federal policy in bilingual education. *Harvard Review, 52*, 149-168.

Rowe, D. W. (1994). Response to McCarthey: The limitations of eclecticism in research. *Reading Research Quarterly, 29*(3), 242-245.

Rumelhart. D. E. & McClelland, J. (Eds.). (1986). *Parallel distributed processing, Vol. 1: Foundations*. Cambridge, MA: MIT Press.

Schieffelin, B. & Cochran-Smith, M. (1984). Learning to read culturally: Literacy before schooling. In H. Goelman, A. Oberg, & F. Smith (eds.), *Awakening to literacy* (3-23). Portsmouth, NH: Heinemann.

Schmidt, P.R. (1993a). Literacy development of two bilingual, ethnic-minority children in a kindergarten program. In D.J. Leu & C.K. Kinzer (Eds.), *Examining central issues in literacy research, theory and practice*. Forty-second yearbook of the National Reading Conference. Chicago, IL: National Reading Conference.

Schmidt, P.R. (1993b). *Cultural conflict and struggle: Literacy learning in a kindergarten program*. Unpublished dissertation, Syracuse University, Syracuse, NY.

Schmidt, P.R. (1995). Working and playing with others: cultural conflict in a kindergarten literacy program. *The Reading Teacher, 48*(5), 404-412.

Schmidt, P.R. (1996a). One teacher's reflections: Implementing multicultural literacy learning. *Equity and Excellence in Education, 29* (2), 20-29. An imprint of Greenwood Publishing Group, Inc., Westport, CT.

Schmidt, P.R. (1996b). Autobiographies, interviews and cross cultural analysis. Symposium paper delivered at annual meeting of National Reading Conference, Charleston, SC, December 4-7.

Schon, D. A. (1983). *The reflective practitioner*. New York: Basic Books, Inc.

Schon, D. A. (1987). *Educating the reflective practitioner*. San Francisco: Jossey-Bass, Inc.

Scheurich, J. J. (1993). Toward a white discourse on White racism. *Educational Researcher, 22(8)*, 5-10.

Skutnabb-Kangas, T. & Cummins, J. (Eds.). (1988). *Minority education: From shame to struggle*. Clevedon, U. K.: Multilingual Matters.

Sleeter, C. E. (Ed.). (1991). *Empowerment through multicultural education*. Albany: SUNY Press.

Snow, C. F. (1992). Perspectives on second language development: Implications for bilingual education. *Educational Researcher, 21(2)*, 16-19.

Spindler, G. (Ed.) (1987). *Doing the ethnography of schooling*. Prospect Heights, IL: Waveland Press.

Spindler, G., & Spindler, L. (1987). *The interpretive ethnography of education: At home and abroad*. Hillsdale, NJ: Lawrence Erlbaum Associates.

Spodek, B. (Ed.). (1986). *Today's kindergarten: Exploring the knowledge base, expanding the curriculum*. New York: Teachers College Press.

Spradley, J. (1979). *The ethnographic interview*. New York: Holt, Rinehart & Winston.

Squires, S. (1993). *Planting the seeds of multiculturalism in an elementary school*. Unpublished master's project in education. Cortland State University, Cortland, New York.

Stuckey, J. E. (1991). *The violence of literacy*. Portsmouth, NH: Boynton/Cook Publishers.

Sulzby, E., & Teale, W. H. (1991). Emergent literacy. In R. Barr, M. Kamil, P. Mosenthal, & P. D. Pearson (Eds.), *Handbook in reading research (Vol.II)*. New York: Longman.

Suess, D. (1968). *The foot book*. New York: Random House.

Swain, M. (1972). Bilingualism as a first language. Unpublished doctoral dissertation. University of California, Irvine.

Swain, M. (1979). Bilingual education: Research and its implications. In C. A. Yorio, K. Perkins, and J. Schachter (Eds.), *On TESOL 79: The learner in focus,* Washington, DC: Teachers of English to Speakers of Other Languages.

Swain, M. (1988). Manipulating and complementing content teaching to maximize second language learning. *TESL/ Canadian Journal, 6*, 78-83.

Tan, A. (1992). Mother tongue. In *Best essays of 1992*. New York: Longman.

Taylor, D. (1983). *Family literacy: Young children learning to read and write*. Exeter, NH: Heinemann.

Taylor, D., & Dorsey-Gaines, C. (1988). *Growing up literate*.

Portsmouth, NH: Heinemann.

Taylor, S., & Bogdan, R. C. (1984). *Introduction to qualitative research methods.* New York: Wiley.

Teale, W. H. (1982). Toward a theory of how children learn to read and write naturally. *Language Arts, 59,* 555-570.

Teale, W. H., & Martinez, M. G. (1989). Fostering emergent literacy in kindergarten children. In J. Mason (Ed.), *Reading and writing connections* (pp. 177-198). Boston: Allyn & Bacon.

Teale, W. H., & Sulzby, E. (1987). Introduction: Emergent literacy as a perspective for examining how young children become writers and readers. In W.H. Teale and E. Sulzby (Eds.), *Emergent literacy.* Norwood, NJ: Ablex.

Trueba, H. T. (1989). *Raising silent voices: Educating the linguistic minorities for the 21st century.* New York: Newbury House Publishers.

Trueba, H. T., Jacobs, L., & Kirton, E. (1990). *Cultural conflict and adaptation: The case of Hmong children in American society.* New York: Falmer Press.

Vacca, J. L. (1989). Staff development. In S. B. Wepner, J. T. Feeley, & D. S. Strickland (Eds.). *The administration and supervision of reading programs.* New York: Teachers College Press.

Vacca, J.L. (Ed.). (1992). *Bringing about change in schools.* Newark, DE: International Reading Association.

Vacca, J. L. (1994). What works for teachers in professional growth and development. *The Reading Teacher, 47* (8), 672-673.

Vandenberg, B. (1981). Environmental and cognitive factors in social play. *Experimental child psychology, 31,* 169-175.

Verhoeven, L. (1987). *Ethnic minority children acquiring literacy.* Providence, RI: Foris Publications.

Vygotsky, L. S. (1978). *Mind in society: The development of higher psychological processes.* Cambridge, MA: Harvard University Press.

Vygotsky, L. S. (1986). *Thought and language.* Cambridge, MA: MIT Press.

Waggoner, D. (1988). Language minorities in the United States in the 1980's: The evidence from the 1980 census. In S.L. McKay and S.C. Wong (Eds.), *Language diversity: Problem or resource* (pp. 66-108). New York: Newbury House Publishers.

Wasley, P. (1991). *Teachers who lead: The rhetoric of reform and the realities of practice.* New York: Columbia Teachers College.

Watts Pailliotet, A. (1994). *Home/School Connection: The vital factor in bilingual, ethnic-minority literacy learning.* Symposium paper, 1994 National Reading Conference 44th Annual Meeting, San Diego, California, November 30-December 3.

Weber, R. (1990). Linguistic diversity and reading in American Society. In R. Barr., M. Kamil, P. Mosenthal, & P. D. Pearson (Eds.), *Handbook on reading research (Vol. II).* New York: Longman.

Wells, G. (1986). *The meaning makers: Children learning language and using language to learn.* Portsmouth, NH: Heinemann Press.

Wong-Fillmore, L. (1983). The language learner as an individual: Implications of research on individual differences for the ESL teacher. In M. A. Clarke & J. Handscombe (Eds.), *On TESOL '82: Pacific perspectives on language learning and teaching* (pp.157-173). Washington DC: TESOL.

Xu, H. (1996). A Filipino ESL kindergartener's successful beginning literacy learning experience in a mainstream classroom. In D. J. Leu, C. K. Kinzer & K.A. Hinchman (Eds.), *Literacies for the 21st Century: Research and Practice.* Forty-fifth yearbook of the National Reading Conference. Chicago, IL: The NRC, Inc.

Zelinsky, P. (1990). *The wheels on the bus.* New York: Dutton.

Index

156

Patricia Ruggiano Schmidt, an early childhood and reading teacher for twenty-five years, earned her doctorate in Reading and Language Arts from Syracuse University. *Cultural Conflict and Struggle: Literacy Learning in a Kindergarten Program* rooted from her dissertation, which received recognition from the International Reading Association in 1994. Dr. Schmidt is Assistant Professor in the Education Department at Le Moyne College, New York, where her research, teaching and service revolve around literacy and multicultural education. In 1996, Dr. Schmidt was honored with the Le Moyne College Matteo Ricci Award for her work and achievements related to campus diversity.